GENERATION BRAND

To my husband, Chris.

Praise for GENERATION BRAND

"*Irina Soriano is boldly taking a stand on gender equity for 'Generation Brand' (those born 2012-2030), introducing new thinking that has a clear link between the need to polish the social media landscape that girls and women are growing up in and empowering them to feel confident, equal to their male counterparts, and ultimately motivated to propel their career path to executive levels. The masses can benefit from the concept of life-brand and mastering it for a fulfilling, fair and just life.*"

—Susan MacKenty Brady, CEO, Simmons University
Institute for Inclusive Leadership

"*In a world of rapid change and innovation, this book is both a wake-up call about the pitfalls accompanying this progress, and a roadmap for using the concept of life-brand as a new tool for social good and personal welfare. Managing your personal information and how it impacts your reputation and life-brand is going to be an essential part of everybody's toolkit. Today, we are able to project our views, beliefs, knowledge, experience, and personalities onto a wide, sometimes even global canvas. Learning to do that safely and effectively is going to be an indispensable skill set for 'Generation Brand' and future generations, both in the workplace and in private settings.*"

—Christopher Willcox, former CEO JP Morgan Asset
Management

"*The book, Generation Brand, is phenomenal. Once upon a time, only adult professionals had to consider all things branding, but now, an entire generation of tech-savvy, 'social' children are being* ushered in. This is an essential guide."

—Maureen Lippe, Founder and Chairman, Lippe Taylor
PR & Digital Marketing

"My childhood was riddled with campaigns reminding us to buckle up in a car, eat healthy and exercise. For the most part it worked. Today there is a new reality with social media and the impact it can have on our kids. Irina Soriano takes a thoughtful and pragmatic approach to this new reality. Most importantly, she provides a blueprint to help us navigate and control our life-brand."

—Matthew Seeley, Executive Vice President, Merkle

"Social media is here to stay, and when we learn to coexist with it mindfully and safely, it can be a powerful tool for influential good. This is why Generation Brand is a must read for anyone engaging online who desires to embrace a future in business, politics or even applying to college. When you are clear on how to show up online, that is in alignment with your brand, what 'shows up' will never be a concern. Generation Brand is a book for the times and required reading for any parent."

—Tricia Brouk, international award-winning director,
author and founder, The Big Talk Academy

"We are now products, dangerously becoming commodities, with girls mostly on the receiving end of a lack of empathy and hate, and without the tools to fight back—making them vulnerable to a destructive spiral of emotional abuse. Generation Brand provides the tools through awareness to take control of your 'life-brand'."

—Marcia Elizabeth Christian Favale, Founder and CEO,
Blingby

GENERATION BRAND

Controlling Your Life-Brand for
Likes, Loves and Career Advancement

Irina Soriano

Contents

IRINA SORIANO

Foreword

When you join two companies, the most important thing is the team, so I spend a lot of time getting to know the people, figuring out who we hold onto, who might be at risk, who will have big impact and what role each person might play. In 2019, when Seismic, a software company focused on sales and marketing enablement, acquired Percolate, Irina Soriano's name came up early and often. As I got to know her, I realized why.

A quick search and it is obvious what Irina cares about. She's passionate about a number of social causes, especially the cause of equity. She's in a critical role promoting the brand of our company and in the unique position of being a highly visible leader in a new field, *sales enablement*. When you look a little deeper, you realize the common thread is brand. She's expertly building her own brand, along with that of our company and the entire field of sales enablement. In essence, I consider her a multidimensional brand expert. She is pioneering a new era of what *brand* actually means.

Brand cannot be defined by simply a company or product any longer. Technology devices and communication mechanisms have played a massive role in what makes us human today, and we look to possibilities and opportunities that help us all thrive.

We are all distinct brands—life-brands, as Irina introduces in her profound book, *Generation Brand*. The book both foretells the considerations of a generation entirely connected and plugged in, technology-wise, and emphasizes the importance of minding our own brands that are hugely dynamic online, real-time.

I recently celebrated a birthday as a proud Gen Xer. I did not grow up with devices. I was first exposed to a computer and started programming in junior high school. It was a non-connected universe. Fast forward a couple of decades, and I found myself with twenty-two ways (I counted!) to connect with me. Phone numbers, fax lines, email addresses, messaging accounts. At that one point, I said, that's enough! I stopped jumping on the next cool thing that came out.

I'm not a huge social user, but I have come to realize that my brand and the company's brand are highly intertwined, and I use social more professionally than personally. My other lens on "connectedness" is through the experience of my kids. I have two boys. My youngest is seventeen and on the autism spectrum. He grew up in the online world and by the time he was ten years old, "online" became the center of his world. He found his community there and most of his friends are people he's never met in person. Some of them he has known for five or six years, pulled together by a shared passion for movies and their VHS and DVD collections. When he was thirteen, some of his friends were nineteen and some were ten, and being protective parents, we paid close attention to who he was interacting with. We saw him make some mistakes and post stuff with bad language or "not good" topics. We helped clean up a couple of messes and helped him learn that what he posts matters and will live with him for many, many years. Now, he's seventeen and tech savvy enough that it's impossible for us to monitor the myriad ways that he can interact. Although we cannot monitor all the connection points, we do our best to help him care for his life-brand.

Life-brand is a critically important topic, and Irina is the right person to own it. In the craziness that was the year of 2020, I learned a lot from her and I'm certain that you will, too. The year was so many things, including a gigantic eye opener to what really matters. It's brought certain groups together, exposing some ugliness and gaps in how we operate as a society. But more importantly, it's brought so many smart, compassionate people together to talk. And read. Read this book...for the good of all life-brands yet to be bred and shaped.

—DOUG WINTER
Co-founder and CEO
Seismic

IRINA SORIANO

Acknowledgements

At the end of 2019, I started to feel that 2020 would be the year I had to step out my comfort zone and invest the additional time outside of my very busy work schedule to make a significant contribution to narrowing the gender gap. A few years back, I met one of the most inspiring, caring, and giving mentors, Pat Wilkinson, who encouraged me to finally bring this work to life. Pat, I am forever thankful for the hours of time you invested to build me up through tough times and all the encouraging words just when I needed them.

Early in 2020, I was introduced to my public speaking and TEDx coach, Tricia Brouk, who since has been instrumental in my journey of manifesting my idea. Tricia, thank you for being passionate about my purpose, and most importantly, filling me with your positivity.

As I embarked on this journey, there were more wonderful people that entered my life. Through Tricia, I met my brilliant editor, Candi Cross, who was instantly hooked by the idea and who has consistently motivated me with her spirit and her patience throughout this process. She did not just have the right sensibility for the topic; she also allowed me to let my personality shine through the huge amount of research that went into the book, so it could be authentic from the beginning to end.

Hollie Hoadley, Jean Pilaprat, Daynna Hartjes, and Alma Wright from Creative Solutions Consulting Inc. have been instrumental in bringing this book to life with their creative ideas, design work and passion about this topic. Thank you for all your effort, input and advice.

This book was written through the global pandemic, while I was stuck on a couch, without an office, sitting in between boxes waiting to move home. I am eternally grateful for our close friends, Chris and Dana Willcox, as well as Matt and Emy Seeley, who have generously let me and my husband stay at their beautiful homes throughout the toughest times of 2020, so I could fully concentrate on this work during late hours and weekends. Words cannot explain how grateful we are to have you all in our lives.

Besides all those direct contributions to my work, there were also many, many career mentors and sponsors (!) that helped me get to where I am today. The person that has been by my side for almost 15 years, provided me with many amazing career opportunities, and always believed in my potential, is Sean Zimdahl. Sean, words cannot express how grateful I am for your friendship and support. You are a very special leader who truly cares for his people. We all felt it over the years!

Another very important boss, mentor, sponsor, and friend is

Stuart Hurwitz. Stuart, thank you for kicking my butt and holding me accountable at all times, which made me a better leader myself. Other sponsors, mentors and supporters have been Abbie Morris, Stuart Ferguson, John Flanigan, Michelle Arieta, Ken Pouliot, Mike Fuss, Ed Calnan, and Toby Carrington. Thank you all for supporting my career journey and for having my back no matter what.

I would also like to thank Doug Winter for contributing the foreword to this book. Doug, it takes compassionate leaders like you to change the landscape for professional women and to close the gender gap for good. I am grateful our paths crossed and that you are supporting my mission to empower the next generation of professional females with such enthusiasm.

Lastly, my family has been the true catalyst behind this work. My parents, Petra and Siegfried, have always pushed me to take risks and to go after what I wanted. I deeply thank you for providing me with your love and support. My sister Joana, a successful, smart, and ambitious CEO and a woman I aspire to be, has not just been a role model for my own career, but more so, an inspiration to know that there is no limit for women that put themselves out there.

And finally, my husband, Chris. I have never met a human being that is more loving, caring, and giving. He has not just been a source of inspiration for this topic; he has also been closely involved in the process to complete this work, inspired me, and gave input and ideas, as well as honest criticism and constructive feedback. There were many times when I was holding back and his constant encouragement to fully "go for it" led me down the path of being truly authentic with everything I do. Without his belief in me as well as his time commitment and support, I would have probably never written this book.

Chris, I love you with all my heart and I am eternally grateful for you giving me the courage to discover all the beautiful things I can do with my life!

BEFORE YOU CONTINUE READING

I want you to take a few minutes and think about the following

- Every comment or post you made and every picture or video you shared on social media since you signed up for your first account.

- Every possible comment, post, picture or video featuring you that someone else shared on social media.

- Every picture or video that was ever taken of you, that people might have on their smart phone or laptop.

- And lastly, every printed photo that someone may have hidden in their drawer that can possibly see the light of day in the future.

Introduction

Your Life-Brand

"There are only two industries that call their customers 'users': illegal drugs and software."

—Edward Tufte, American Statistician and Professor, Yale University

I wonder how the last five minutes went and how you feel right now. When I did this thinking exercise for the first time, I did some rough math. I had my first Facebook account at the age of

23; that means 13+ years of comments, posts, and likes. I do all three of these things probably 10 times a day, that's over 3,650 contributions per year and almost 47,500 social media interactions over the last 13 years—only via my Facebook account, and which does not include what others posted about me.

This is a hell lot of content I surely do not remember. No matter how many years you spent accumulating posts, likes, pictures, and videos, how could you possibly know everything that is out there about you? Do you remember what pictures or video others took of you when you had a couple of drinks too many? It's out there regardless of your recollection. If not on someone's phone, your precarious image is buried under some old documents in a school friend's drawer or packed in someone's memory box in their closet. Maybe that person is not your friend anymore or holds a grudge against you these days. It could be a disaster waiting to happen.

If you own a phone, I am sure it is near you right now. You use it so much that you've been guilty of looking for it while you're holding it! RescueTime tells us that the average adult swipes, clicks, types, and makes calls over the course of 3 hours and 15 minutes each day (the top 20% even spend 4.5 hours on their phones). In other words, 50 days per year full of opportunity to make a mistake and post or comment something you might regret later in life. Maybe it will cost you your education or your job. Maybe it will cost you your family. Or if you are lucky, it won't cost you anything but data charges, and you will be just fine.

Milwaukee Brewers baseball pitcher Josh Hader had to learn the hard way that every word counts, when several tweets from his account from 2011 surfaced seven years later with one saying: "I hate gay people." Hader was 17 and 18 years old when he tweeted this and other statements of that same nature. The twisted tweeting did not end his career yet damaged his reputation.

Justine Sacco, on the other hand, did lose her job over one single tweet. In 2013, the then 30-year-old public relations executive boarded an eleven-hour flight from London to South Africa posting on Twitter just before taking off: "Going to Africa. Hope I don't get AIDS. Just kidding. I'm white!" While she was in the air, a viral Twitter storm ensued, surprising her with a globally trending hashtag stating *#HasJustineLandedYet* and a damaged reputation. She lost her job the following day. Her name—and a dark cloud—surface on Twitter even now.

Following stories like Sacco's and Hader's, we often hear that posting did not happen with intention and it was not meant to come off a certain way. Speaking of intention, ask yourself the following:

- Have you ever posted without intention?

- Have you ever posted out of emotion?

- Have you ever posted drunk?

If the answer is "yes" or "maybe" to any of those questions, I would go back to the beginning of this book and turn the five minutes into a couple of hours browsing through all your social media accounts to gain an understanding of just how unintentional your lifetime content library might be.

You need only look to a slew of movies released that reflect our digital culture: "Share" revolves around a teenage girl navigating the fallout after discovering a disturbing cell phone video. "The Social Dilemma" is about tech experts sounding the alarm on the dangerous human impact of social networking and how we have "become the product". In "Spree", desperate for an online following, a rideshare driver figures out a deadly plan to go viral and he will stop at nothing to get his five minutes of fame. (This one particularly freaks me out considering how often I rideshare in New York City!) And if these aren't all ominous enough, "Host" centers on six friends who accidentally invite the attention of a demonic presence during an online séance and begin noticing strange occurrences in their homes.

Generation Brand is not a movie. It is a playbook for taking control of what I have coined your "life-brand", so you can *arrive, advance,* and *thrive* in the professional corridors of your career and livelihood instead of potentially tarnishing your education and career, because nobody prepared you for what could come after opening the social media flood gates through your first Facebook, Instagram, TikTok or Twitter account.

life-brand
[/lIEf/ /brAnd/]

noun

> an individual's digital fingerprint shaped by the collection of publicly accessible content shared by or featuring the individual such as photos, videos, audio recordings, social media posts, and written statements or comments.

Life-brand literally has a life of its own if not controlled by us—it gains power and strength over a lifetime the more content you accumulate in the cloud (or on paper, if you grew up with Kodak cameras like me). We all possess *one* life-brand. It might be strong, or it might be weak, but our individual life-brand exists. *Generation Brand* will teach you how to control your life-brand and understand what shape life-brand can take over different stages.

Screen time is no longer a casual activity. A click, a post—in one breath—can stain, even sustain, your reputation just like that. However, if you frame your life as your *life-brand*, which I will show you how to do, you will indeed, be able to use social media as the tool it was originally designed for, instantly recognize when it could harm you and thwart the danger. I certainly don't mean harm in the form of a "demonic presence" like the movie "Host"! Still, we'll look at a few striking cases of tarnished reputations.

In my efforts, I focus on two gigantic dilemmas, and one will feed the other: Uncontrolled social media usage and the lack of gender parity in the workplace. At first blush, these dilemmas do not seem to be related, but as you come on the life-brand journey with me, you will learn that both of those huge challenges actually have *one thing* in common: They are the solution to one another.

Glimpse into a Life-Brand

I grew up in a small town in Germany, alongside a sister six years older. I know it's rare to say these days, but I had a drama-free, happy family life in an upper-middleclass upbringing. I had loving parents that instilled early confidence and self-belief in me from a young age.

I started my first job in London and this experience took me to Singapore where I met my wonderful husband on a random night at a bar. Marrying a New Yorker determined my path to follow him home. My dream of becoming a New Yorker just like Carrie Bradshaw in "Sex and the City", my favorite show as teenager, finally came true.

There is a bridge between me going through those experiences in Europe, Asia, and the United States, after growing up in a small town in Germany. I studied and worked in a lot of countries, taking in the diverse cultural acumen, reading between the lines of foreign languages, and also, picking up on the differences and similarities of girls and women. My journey allowed me to discover my own life-brand in my early thirties that was firstly built upon my profession and is now also centered around my passion in life—making a significant contribution to closing the gender gap. My experiences are what I like to call my "brand and butter"!

I am also a Millennial. And just so you have a bit more context for who is talking to you, I would like to share a list of descriptors associated with our age range. I consider some of them

factual, others, mere opinion. But in the end, people's perceptions count in the social media realm and the business arena.
This is key throughout *Generation Brand*.

Millennials were born between 1981 and 1996, and we've
also been called the "Entitlement" generation. Millennials are
generally associated with the following:

- Grew up with communication devices

- More ethnically and racially diverse, more culturally and
  racially tolerant

- Optimistic, impatient, entrepreneurial

- Short attention span

- Acceptant of change

- Un-trusting of "the man"

- Achievement-oriented and financially savvy

- Want instant gratification

- Search for the individual who will help them achieve their
  goals

- Want open, constant communication and positive rein-
  forcement from their boss

- Search for job that provides great, personal fulfillment

- Work to live, rather than live to work

- Rise of the Internet, CDs/DVDs

Which of these descriptors would I personally agree with? It does not matter. As tempting as it may be, I will not say. All of these factors heavily contribute to Millennials' life-brands because at minimum, others' impressions and perceptions count. We may be either reinforcing or countering a popular impression or perception at any time. We are one of the "fortunate" generations to being introduced to social media later in life, not on day one. I often wonder how much more unintentional content I would have accumulated if I had a smart phone and social media access at 11 years old, like most American kids do these days, according to the *Common Sense Report*. If you are reading this book and you are from a generation previous to Millennials, what do you think your life would be like today, if all the stupid shit you did back then with your friends, was now publicly available on Facebook, Instagram or Twitter? The thought is quite frankly, terrifying.

To all parents reading this book (most of you likely also got introduced to social media at a more mature age): How worried or aware are you that your child could make *one* mistake that could cost them their entire education and career?

These days, kids are handed smartphones and access to the Internet at the age of 11, or when they are just about to start middle school. Teens aged 16 to 18 years old in the US say they started using social channels around 14 years old, and nearly a third say they even started before the age of 13. If you are providing your kids and young adolescents with a smartphone connected to the world before they have the maturity to navigate the roads of social media in a responsible way without exposing themselves and others to possible harm, it is like letting them drive a car way before having reached the legal driving age. It's freakin' dangerous (or add your own F-word)!

As many parental controls you set up to ensure your child's account is "private", note that it only needs one push of a button for a photo or video to make its way outside of that private account into the world's public social pages, being accessible to 3.8 billion smart phone users in an instant. I know it's hard to believe, but yes, 3.8 BILLION! If that is not horrifying as a parent, then I really don't know what is. There is no protection for your child, unless we ensure the concept of life-brand and the consequences of not controlling it at a young age are understood *before* that first social media account is created.

Early this year, my husband and I attended a social gathering at our friend's home (yes, we did those things pre-pandemic), and I chatted with a neighbor about writing this book. He said, "I keep telling my 16-year-old daughter to not post anything on social media that includes people consuming alcohol, too much skin, or any inappropriate behavior for her age. And she doesn't give a crap about what I am saying. I can only trust she is smart enough not to do anything stupid. Maybe she needs to hear it from someone else other than her dad." This conversation made me even more motivated to write this book. The pressure, especially on girls and young women these days, is immense and social media is not lifting any of it. On the contrary.

As part of the research for this book, I allowed time to chat with young women about their social media experiences and how these impact their day-to-day. One conversation with a 19-year-old particularly struck a nerve with me. She candidly said, "There is so much hate on social. Last year, I shared my one and only TikTok video wearing a bathing suit and I got so much hate. I didn't want to wear a bathing suit ever again and I am a lifeguard."

I don't think I am wrong to declare that women, in general, take things more to heart than men, which can have a huge impact on one's confidence if you receive a lot of criticism through social media. I notice it about myself, how much self-love and confidence it takes to become immune to hate, criticism, and flat-out mean and unnecessary comments in the real and virtual world. It requires one to stand behind how you express yourself and to be intentional about what you share on social media. Controlling your life-brand will allow you to do just that. And yet, it still occasionally hits me. I recently received a comment in French on a professional post that featured me and my work saying that "my head was huge", that "I should stop getting so much plastic surgery" and that this "made me look ugly". While this comment was not just stupid, mean, and outright ridiculous (I am in my mid-thirties), I was upset about it all day. And considering what comments some of my peers receive, this wasn't even that bad. My point is, when you are active on social media these days, you will get criticism and comments that you will not enjoy, and they will make you feel bad. It's part of the game. The key is to know how to handle backlash and how to stand behind what you are sharing, so it feeds your confidence rather than destroying it.

Reaction Culture—Live or Die...Online

I talked to a popular high school principal at an alternative school in Kansas recently. She said, "Response culture leaves no room for no likes or no response." That comment really stuck with me. Getting a response to a social media post is like addiction. And with addiction comes a build-up of tolerance. Especially girls and young women that develop early "like-addiction" have the pressure to post more sexy, daring or controversial content, even if this contrasts to who they actually are and misrepresents their true identity and belief. All they are doing is chasing more likes to feed their growing addiction. Maybe the first post received 20 likes. As content gets more controversial, maybe 60 or 70 likes show up. This easily leads to thinking, *how can I get 100 likes*?

Two side effects accompany addiction. Just like any other addiction, chasing likes needs to be fed, which increases the chance to make a severe mistake and share content that might be life-mangling, as well as a possible influx of hate comments, criticism, and cyberbullying. What makes the recipe for disaster even more spicy is a lack of social media education, or at least some sort of guideline on how to handle each. The risk of responding to comments driven by emotion fueling the "hate-fire" arises. It is the start of a vicious viral cycle. The result can be a rapid accumulation of life-brand content that cannot be corrected or erased ("delete" on social media does not mean someone else hasn't already taken a screenshot) and shattered self-confidence that might significantly impact one's future career. Like-addiction can leave confidence-scars for life.

This next generation entirely born in the 21st century is growing up with these problems, as it has become everyday life. But we know that's not *life* in its pure sense. Life is ups and downs and management of them, relationships, resilience, the quest for fulfillment, being of service, love, impact. It's simply so much more than the battle between instant gratification and one mistake and everything going downhill.

For girls and young women, it's even harder because they are three times more likely to be exposed to cyberbullying than boys and young men. Following girls who have experienced bullying through their evolution, education, and career, I am certain you see the child who can't concentrate enough to learn and then the young female who can't ask for a promotion or a salary increase. An early lack of confidence and self-belief will impact a woman's life tremendously—at minimum, her ability to drive her career and to show up confidently equal to her male peers when it's time to climb the career ladder.

For the record, I'm a woman that is *pro* social media. I have a solid followership and I learned to embrace it later in life—the good, the bad, and the ugly. Most importantly, I learned what skills it can teach me, how they serve me to enhance my career, and how social media helped me strengthen my confidence and self-belief. Once I discovered life-brand for myself, I started to embrace social media in a controlled and safe way. I've learned that your life-brand voice can drive change and set the example for others. With more and more people, especially women, embracing this concept and actively controlling their own life-brands, girls will be able to join the social media highway seeing different examples of women of all ages posting intentionally about things they care about and that truly represents them, as well as their chosen purpose. Let's face it: Social media is not going away and our only chance to change the landscape for the next generation is to actively embrace it, use it to build our confidence and professional skill sets, and to have some fun, also.

Many playbooks taut 100 or even 250 skills that leaders possess. Well, I say that besides kindness and caring for other humans, communication, relationship building, influencing, and integrity are pretty much all you need to successfully make it to the top. I did not have the opportunity to use social media to shape these skills early on, but I developed them later in life, thanks to career experiences and controlling my own life-brand. These skills have equipped me to be in the driver's seat of my career and to create opportunities for myself in the workplace and in life.

Think of *Generation Brand* as a fresh perspective on how to embrace social media and use it in a safer and controlled way so it propels your confidence and lifts you up rather than tearing you down. Besides the different scenarios of life-brand, I will explain how it enables every human with social media access to impact positive change in their life and our society over the course of a lifetime. That goes for women and men.

If we are using social media, we might as well capitalize on it. In my book (figuratively and literally), capitalizing on it is being aware of our life-brand, its impact on our future, and the potential it has to allow women and men to close the gender gap in the workplace together for good, creating full gender equality. If you don't know how social media protocol and gender equity can be intertwined, you will have no doubt after devouring *Generation Brand*! You will walk away being inspired to actively control your life-brand through social media, understand the consequences of unintentional behavior and language on your life-brand, and most importantly, pass on this knowledge to young people in your life to help drive gender equality in the workplace through protecting them from an "out-of-control" life-brand that could ruin their bright future.

Generation Brand promises lessons on:

- The concept of a controlled, uncontrolled, and misaligned life-brand.

- How to create a strong life-brand voice in the world impacting significant positive change.

- Getting *likes* and *loves* posting content on social media that is aligned to your identity.

- Using life-brand to build confidence, self-belief and awareness, as well as critical leadership skills at an early age.

- **For the females amongst us**: how to use life-brand to uniquely position yourself to take on career opportunities in the workplace feeling equal to your male counterparts.

This book will not bring a stop to like-addiction. If you are active on social media you will be a victim of it to some degree, I can speak for myself. The goal is to ensure your addiction is not screwing up your life, but rather, enables you to develop strong confidence and belief in yourself and your abilities.

Understanding the concept of life-brand has the potential to create a paradigm shift in gender equality for several generations: Millennials (born between 1981-1995), Generation (or Gen) Z (born after 1996), and especially the following generation entirely born in the 21st century. My mission is to enable females to take ownership of narrowing the gender gap in the workplace through controlling their life-brands, but gender parity can only be achieved if men and women of all ages work together on a future of equal opportunities, free of gender bias and barriers of career advancement to senior leadership. Gender equality requires equal efforts from both to become reality, and while men and women probably take different things away from it, the education of life-brand should be offered to both from an early age.

So, come along. And be a part of shaping a whole new era.

1

The Death of Privacy

"Everybody wants to be a celebrity, which is why we have this phenomenon of social media, where nobody wants to be private. We all want to be seen."

—Marc Jacobs, American fashion designer

Human beings are wired and connected starting with their parents posting about their infantile narrative. Kids are surely not asked for their "consent" to be featured on social media these days. As a woman in her mid-thirties knowing what I know today, I would not be delighted to know that my parents had posted a collection of images and videos of me online using the potty for the first time or holding a glass of wine as a 2-year-old with the caption "#WineBaby" or slurring inappropriate language in the camera after having my wisdom teeth taken out.

Lucky for me, my parents did not have access to social media when I grew up, and in hindsight, I am thankful for that. Children with Millennial or Gen Z parents are facing a much different reality these days being featured on social media possibly from the day they are born. Personally, I do not consider it a violation of privacy to post pictures and videos of your children at an age where they cannot give their consent to be featured, but the question quickly arises where to draw the line. These pictures or videos will very likely not cost them a job later in life, but social media exposure through parents means life-brand now starts to bloom with that first photo or video shared. It also means many years of uncontrolled and unintentional life-brand building, an accumulation of content in the cloud that will remain there forever, even if deleted. And it definitely means we are taking the control away from children to have full control of their life-brand due to the hundreds or thousands pieces of content that feature them online until they even understand what this all means.

Also, social media activity by parents now becomes an example for kids and young adults. We know that kids are handed smartphones and access to the Internet at the age of 11 these days, reports "Uploaded" by *Common Sense Report*. That's when they are just about to start middle school. And again, 16- to 18-year-olds in the US say they started using social channels around 14 years old, and nearly a third say they even started before the age of 13. A lack of life-brand awareness by parents and kids will heavily impact this generation's future life-brands in the years to come.

Gen Z has been officially recognized by analysts such as PEW Research Center as kids and young adults born after 1996. Interestingly, the generation following Gen Z, children born after 2012, has not been officially defined yet. Gen Alpha started to appear as a definition for the generation born entirely in this century but has never been adopted by analysts as an official name at this stage. You will hear me referring to this specific group of kids and future young adults as "Generation Brand" throughout this book. Generation Brand is growing up with smartphone and social media access from day one of their lives. This generation will be defined by their life-brands; they will either become a victim of it, or, with the right education, they can be the most powerful generation to ever have lived.

What intensifies life-brand for Generation Brand even more is the current COVID-19 pandemic driving more and more social media and video-based interactions as a result of a lack of face-to-face social connections. Let's take a look at some of the possible challenges and components of daily life facing Generation Brand in the years to come:

- Increased daily social media usage and screen time

- Job and financial insecurity post-COVID-19 pandemic

- Cybersecurity and data breaches

- Free flow of misinformation about important topics such as health, travel, civility and government

- In business, changing patterns of customer behavior, with more human interaction taking place online (I honestly thought that the ability to buy a car on Amazon and a house on a phone app was pretty groundbreaking, so I can only imagine what we're in.)

- Self-driving vehicles, more robots, extended and augmented reality

- Massive biodiversity loss and resource use; climate change

- Changing disease patterns

I am not trying to paint a picture of doom here, as I also believe—and trends show—that Generation Brand will have more ideas and ingenuity, more empathy, diversity & inclusion and authenticity, more technology and R & D, and more resources overall to solve global challenges for generations to come. With that, life-brands must be intact, so every single mind and reputation is strong.

Constant Visibility

Almost half of the world's population now owns a smartphone and we know for a fact that "people in advanced economies are more likely to have mobile phones (smartphones in particular) and are more likely to use the Internet and social media than people in emerging economies" according to PEW Research.

Teenagers spend an average of seven hours and 22 minutes on their phones, followed by 8- to 12-year-olds with four hours and 44 minutes. Yes, that's right, *every single day*. These stats tell us one thing: no matter what we do or say when another person is around us, our actions can technically reach, be shared, and consumed by the world (not just smartphone users) at any point in time. Besides our own smartphone, the chances for another device to be in the room with us are incredibly high, meaning there could be full visibility and documentation of any displayed behavior or language through video or capturing an image without our consent or permission that might be broadcasted to the world in an instant. With data now being accessible almost everywhere through smartphones, online content now gets viewed, shared, and commented on almost instantly, leading to content possibly going "viral" at an incredible rate. Especially unacceptable and controversial content can quickly lead to creating a mainstream of negative opinion about the content itself, the language, the behavior, or the person leading to what is now called "cancel culture", which we will cover more in-depth.

Consider this fact: A simple comment or behavior that might seem insignificant, meaningless, funny, or "a good idea at the time" can destroy a person's life and future with the simple click of a button, ruining their reputation and life-brand possibly forever. The ironic thing is, at its core, "sharing" used to be a good practice to live by!

My husband and I are spending a lot of time with friends who have daughters that are 19 years old or so, and often hear them say "All I post is in a private account." It does not occur to them that anybody with access to said private account can copy, record, and screenshot anything they want. There seems to be a general level of trust towards the people that were given access to our private accounts. The issue is that friends can also make mistakes, friends can turn sour or jealous, and things might slither out of the privacy of those accounts.

The COVID-19 pandemic has even heightened our daily visibility and taken the lack of privacy to a whole new level. With offices being closed and many of us working from the privacy of our homes, video-based interactions now ask for most of us to let others into our private living space (that is if you haven't figured out how to use a virtual video background). And this scenario has exposed a whole new range of possible life-brand missteps that we never imagined before. I am referring to the gentleman who appeared butt naked on a video work call with colleagues only noticing his camera was on after exposing his front and back from several angles to his peers. Or the young lady on a work call, who had to use the restroom and decided to take her laptop with her while doing so to ensure she was not missing any of the conversation. Very likely accidents that were followed by serious life-brand contamination! I can't help but thinking how a job interview would go, when your future boss has access to you walking around naked on a work video call with colleagues, exposing yourself to the camera. Would you hire this gentleman to work for you?

There are also more famous personalities that found themselves in situations of full display of private moments shared on camera. A recent example is author and CNN commentator Jeffrey Toobin, who has been suspended from *The New Yorker* after exposing his penis and masturbating during a work call. The incident received very different reactions, from some finding it sad to some thinking it was funny. According to FOX News, Toobin issued an apology, stating, "I made an embarrassingly stupid mistake, believing I was off-camera. I apologize to my wife, family, friends and co-workers," […] "I believed I was not visible on Zoom. I thought no one on the Zoom call could see me. I thought I had muted the Zoom video." I will not comment on the fact that the apology was for being seen and heard during this solitaire moment, and not for displaying this action during a *work* call. What do you think?

And let's not forget about all the kids that had to become video-tool specialists overnight to be "virtually-schooled" while enjoying the safety of their homes. This situation has brought a new level of visibility but also exposure to the youngest amongst us. Recent examples of random pornographic, violent, or racist content being dropped in video classrooms by hackers are a severe safety concern. The even bigger issue is, taking into account the concept of digital content accumulation shaping children's life-brands from an early age, is that every wrong word said, or every inappropriate behavior displayed is not only videotaped, but is making its way into the cloud where it is stored forever. Kids make mistakes, kids react out of emotion, kids do not act with intention at all times, and that's okay. We learn as we grow. But the current generation of virtually educated kids do not have the freedom to be kids, and if they choose to do so, it'll now be documented and recorded.

There are dynamics at play molding life-brands that we did not have to consider pre-pandemic. Life is…well, rather shared and intimate in the year 2020.

While conceptualizing this book, I told my husband that I don't know the pile of crap we've accumulated in the last twenty years on social and beyond. "We are probably already screwed anyways, make sure others know better!" he insisted. If you are reading this book, I hope the least you will take away is a level of consciousness around life-brand. You can share the awareness with children and young adults in your life, so they can avoid possible missteps. Maybe you even decide to actively control your life-brand and work the life-brand game as you are in school or at work.

If the latter, stay tuned for the "Life-Brand Launch Kit" at the end of this book, which you can start using while reading to kick off your exciting life-brand journey in real time.

Confidence Hacks

Do something that scares you today. Is it talking to a stranger who seems interesting? Working out at a gym after a long time? Exploring your creative self through writing a poem, song or short story? Dressing differently?

Stepping out of your comfort zone is imperative to boosting confidence.

2

Chasing the Like

"When you get to a place where you understand that love and belonging, your worthiness, is a birthright and not something you have to earn, anything is possible."

—Brené Brown, American professor, author, and lecturer

D o you have your coffee with your social media feed in the morning? I sometimes do. Maybe even two cups.

Depending on your platform of choice it could be Facebook,

Twitter, Instagram, or TikTok. Whichever platform we're on, one of the first checkpoints is the 'notification' tab. 'Has anyone liked my post'? 'Has anyone tagged me'? It's a habit we quickly get pulled into.

When your post attracts more likes than normal, a little rush bubbles up inside. There is a reason for that rush. For every thumbs up or heart, we receive a psychological high through a shot of dopamine. The more likes, the more shots. The more shots we have, the more shots we need. Addiction. We're in a reward-seeking loop. That loop grabs for more achievement, purchases, and Instagram. Pick your pleasure.

Social media has significantly grown in popularity, with now about 72% of Americans being active on social, reports PEW Research Center, while only 5% of Americans had a social media account in 2005. As part of the same study, they found that 18-29-year-olds were the most active on social media with 90% usage, closely followed by 30-49-year-olds. It is also important to note that females are posting, liking, and swiping more than men with 78% to 65% respectively and especially platforms like Instagram and Facebook see generally more activity by females versus males.

With young females dominating the social media space, the question becomes why females are more active, and what is the potential impact on them, their self-belief and their confidence levels? There are a couple of somewhat provocative hypotheses to be made about why women, especially in their twenties, are the most active on social media these days.

My first hypothesis is that women might have a higher drive to receive instant gratification, rewards, and recognition through their social media presence and interactions chasing "likes". Acquiring a "like" can lead to an instant feeling of visibility ultimately leading to a short-lived confidence boost. In the first-of-its-kind study scanning teens' brains while using social media, UCLA revealed that eating chocolate, winning money, and accumulating social media "likes" or seeing other people's "likes" activates the same positive neurological responses in young females.

"When the teens saw their own photos with a large number of likes, we saw activity across a wide variety of regions in the brain," said lead author Lauren Sherman, a researcher in the brain mapping center and the UCLA branch of the Children's Digital Media Center. And I thought it was the caffeine lighting my brain up!

Chasing "likes" may also trigger the need to improve one's social media performance by gaining more followers, pushing girls and young women towards posting more risky or controversial content in order to get attention and attract followership.

My second hypothesis is that women might possess a stronger innate need to be liked than men. To be clear, a never-ending *desire* to be liked, not actually being liked, can be problematic. Most normal human beings crave love and belonging. But there is an assumption to be made that young females might have significantly higher social media usage chasing virtual likes, because of this need. The choice of how to obtain the like is what we examine when we are referring to "life-brand".

The Social Road Rage

While social media usage can be extremely powerful especially in the hands of young adults, it can also have significant negative effects that are opposite to the desired outcome, especially for girls and young women.

We know that social media interactions can lead to a negative self-image. A 2018 study by York University revealed that young females interacting with a more attractive peer on social media experienced an "increase in negative body image" while females engaging with a family member did not have this perception. "The findings suggest that upward appearance comparisons on social media may promote increased body image concerns in young adult women."

The increased usage of social media and mental removal from the real world can also lead to isolation, loneliness, and lack of social network and structure with other humans in one's surroundings. The social media community may slowly replace in-person interactions leading down a path of lacking social skills, being uncomfortable and insecure in the real-world, an inability to deal with conflict, and a diminished self-confidence impacted by how one's self-perception is shaped through social media. A damaged self-confidence positions young females unfavorably to start and complete their educational path, entering the workforce, and especially advancing their careers.

Finally, and most importantly, chasing "likes" and attention can lead to the temptation to publish controversial content with the goal of "going viral". Making statements or publishing images or videos that are unseen, socially not acceptable, or insulting to certain groups or minorities with the intention to gain broader attention not just from followers, but also people that share content on other platforms to increase visibility, has resulted in many scorned life-brands.

It has become clear that social media influence in recent years had a strong impact on Generation Brand (born after 2012), the generation following Gen Z. With iPhones and tablets replacing some of the previous generation's toys, early social media usage and exposure to peers and people has resulted in non-stop connection to the world. Even though Pew Research substantiates exact percentages, it's no surprise that 59% of U.S. teens have been bullied or harassed online these days. In addition, almost 37% of kids aged between 12 and 17 have had a bully target them at least once in their lifetime and almost 70% of children that have gone through online harassment have experienced mental health issues. The reason that Cyberbullying.org, which has provided us with some of these nifty stats, even exists is due to the impact of this harassment on mental health. The effects include stress, depression, anxiety, and loss of empathy, amongst others. And girls have it the hardest—they are three times more likely to be bullied than boys. Here, I will provoke the thought of all of those young girls growing up to be career women. Do you think they will forget these experiences as a result of their age? Not exactly. Trauma festers. Hence, the intertwinement between themes you are beginning to see.

Thinking about the children of Generation Brand, it raises a lot of concern how the social media trend is impacting their future and specifically what characteristics, attitudes, and behaviors will be developed under the influence of social media. With females being the most active users and that being unlikely to change for future generations, the growing social media trend poses significant risk:

- Exposure to negative influence and bullying with strong negative impact on a female's early self-awareness and confidence

- Missteps sharing content with possible severe consequences such as criticism and possibly cancel culture

- Unintentional behavior and language being exposed at any point in time and possibly be shared online limiting future career options and advancement to leadership in an already male dominated workplace

If you still feel that the definition of bullying is a grey area or subjective, consider this: In 2014, the *Centers for Disease Control and Department of Education* released the first *federal* definition of bullying. The definition includes three core elements:

- Unwanted aggressive behavior

- Observed or perceived power imbalance

- Repetition or high likelihood of repetition of bullying behaviors

This definition helps determine whether an incident is bullying or any other type of aggressive behavior, such as one-time physical fights, online arguments, or incidents between adults. Some bullying actions can fall into criminal categories, such as harassment, hazing, or assault. I am going to go ahead and connect the dots that CDC felt bullying was such a grave concern as a result of the cyberspace incidents that they deemed bullying prevention a need of public health and a growing research field that investigates the complexities and consequences of bullying. One of the top areas for more research is the prevalence of cyberbullying in online spaces.

Bridging the Divide

Cyberbullying ties into life-brand cultivation and how it can damage the life-brand journey, especially for girls and young women. Research has shown that there is a confidence gap between women and men that significantly impacts how women drive and manage their careers compared to their male counterparts and this is true for the current generation of women in the workplace. Research also suggested that female confidence builds with age and experience, over the course of a life-time. Taking that into account, technically speaking, a professional woman like myself is already at a disadvantage when it comes to advancing my career to senior leadership and executive positions compared to my male peers by confidence-default. We know that companies have to make changes to the work environment to provide equal career opportunities to women across all levels of the organization, but if I still lack the confidence and the self-belief to ask for what I deserve, to take risks, to put myself out there and go for opportunities that I might not be "ready for yet", just like my male counterparts would, closing the gender gap will remain wishful thinking.

If we think about girls and young women of Generation Brand, that have grown up with social media since day one of their lives, and the mental impact social media already had on their Millennial and Gen Z parents, we are looking at a generation that exposes their possibly already lowered self-confidence to cyber-bullying, backlash, and criticism with little to no education on how to act, react, and digest such attacks on the self. The expectation for future women of Generation Brand to enter their educational path and the workforce with strong self-belief is unattainable if the social media landscape they are growing up in remains as is. As it stands currently, studies have shown that social media is negatively impacting girls and young women's development and therefore important traits such as their self-belief. If anything, I would expect the gender gap to even widen as more and more women enter the workforce, if we are not addressing this challenge right now.

The word, *confidence*, comes from the Latin word "fidere" and means "to trust". In a nutshell it enables us to:

- Feel good about ourselves

- Accept our body and mind

- Have self-esteem

- Have trust and belief in our abilities and skills

Confidence gives us courage. It allows us to create opportunities for ourselves, to move out of our comfort zone, and to deal with criticism in a way that does not harm our self-belief. The current social media landscape is not in support of increased female self-confidence, there is no protocol and there are no guardrails for protection that allow young women to use social media as a tool to boost their confidence rather than destroy it. When girls and young women maneuver the social media highway by themselves, it's an accident waiting to happen (and let's pray it's not a life-changing one).

Consider the awareness and education of life-brand as a driver's manual for a controlled social media road trip. A manual that keeps you safe and sound understanding the rules of the virtual world while having the freedom to express yourself and your identity to build your confidence through social channels and beyond. Furthermore, it allows you to understand the possible dangers of getting behind the social media "wheel" and the importance to wear your seat belt, so you can control your social media life-brand with purpose and intention.

Confidence Hacks

Maintain positivity. Stay away from toxic people, or "energy thieves", in real life and on social media. Know the difference! What tears you down and what lifts you up? Do people drain your energy or do they make you feel good about yourself?

IRINA SORIANO

3

All Shame, No Fame?

"Social media made you all way too comfortable with disrespecting people and not getting punched in the face for it."

—Mike Tyson, former world heavyweight champion

We just went from constant visibility, to like-addiction, to cyberbullying and mental disease. Doesn't sound like a fun book to read just yet? Here is the bad news—we are not done.

With social media interactions steadily growing, a new phenomenon has emerged called "cancel culture". Cancel culture refers to the damage of an individual's life-brand by displaying or using inappropriate or unacceptable behavior or language, ultimately leading to social pressure to terminate one's career or education to teach "a lesson" and "punish" for such behavior.

There are numerous examples of cancel culture for all generations that demonstrate the impact behavior can have on your life-brand. A recent example is Amy Cooper, a non-famous white woman walking her unleashed dog in Central Park in New York City when Christian Cooper, a passionate bird-watcher and Harvard graduate, asked her to put her dog on the leash. After refusing to do so, Ms Cooper called 9-1-1 filing a false police report saying an "Africa-American man" was threatening her. According to the *New York Times*, the video of Ms Cooper was watched over 30 million times on social media, her name was trending on Twitter, she received the nickname "Central Park Karen", and lost her dog and employment, leading to her publicly apologizing for her behavior. Several petitions were initiated, calling for NYPD to force Cooper's arrest for making a false police report; one petition having over 18,000 signatures at the time.

If you're not convinced of cancel culture's reach, I'll let opinion columnist Ross Douthat, writing for *The New York Times*, opine on it: "Cancel culture is most effective against people who are still rising in their fields, and it influences many people who don't actually get canceled.

"The point of cancellation is ultimately to establish norms for the majority, not to bring the stars back down to earth. So, a climate of cancellation can succeed in changing the way people talk and argue and behave even if it doesn't succeed in destroying the careers of some of the famous people that it targets. You don't need to cancel Rowling if you can cancel the lesser-known novelist who takes her side; you don't have to take down the famous academics who signed *Harper's Magazine* famous letter attacking cancel culture if you can discourage people half their age from saying what they think. The goal isn't to punish everyone, or even very many someone's; it's to shame or scare just enough people to make the rest conform." The situation he is referring to regarding Harry Potter author J.K. Rowling is that she was one of 150 public figures to denounce cancel culture as an assault on free speech in a signed letter that *Harper's Magazine* published. Rowling came under fire in 2019 after tweeting support for Maya Forstater, a researcher who lost her job after tweeting a series of transphobic comments, according to NBC News. Her tweets received backlash and criticism from many showing their support for the LGBTQ+ community.

Generation Brand: Rogue Role Models

While Ms. Cooper is an established adult professional, there are other examples of cancel culture. Especially 2020 has been a year with many permanent life-brand catastrophes due to a lack of awareness of the impact words and behaviors have and what public perception and backlash it can create.

In early 2020, a teenager living in Gilbert, Arizona, posted a Tik Tok that received severe criticism due to its racist nature. After realizing this misstep, the teen tried to delete the video, but it was already copied and shared on Twitter with over 4 million views. The teen recorded an apology explaining that she was not understanding the impact of her social media post and that she was just looking for more "likes" and apologizing for her misstep, stating to *12news*: "I didn't mean for it to come up as racist even though considering the context of it, I didn't mean it like that, I was just doing a TikTok trend."

In July 2020, a Cornell football recruit came under fire after someone posted a video of him using racial slurs on Twitter, mocking the death of George Floyd (George Perry Floyd Jr. was an African American man killed during an arrest in Minneapolis, US). According to The *Cornell Daily Sun*, the video cost him his place with the University's football team. Andy Noel, Cornell

University's director of athletics and physical education, said: "… There is no room for this behavior in Cornell Athletics." Over 450 signatures were gathered on an online petition calling for his expulsion.

In June 2020, the actress-writer Skai Jackson shared a Twitter post with a young man screaming into the camera using the N-word, and revealed his name, university, field of study, and Instagram handle. The post received over 700,000 views and 5,000 retweets.

Circumstances and motivation displaying behavior publicly vary from case to case. There is no debate that any of these examples of displayed behavior and language are unacceptable and repulsive. But this further demonstrates a clear lack of consciousness of what significant impact documented behavior can have on one's life-brand, education, career, and family due to the vast reach of social media channels. Cancel culture has raised many people's concern on being cancelled over what, may at least seem at the time, "just a stupid tweet", a "joke", or a "loss of temper".

As we move to the next part of this book, we will explore what it means to act and speak with intention and being aware of the weight and impact our behavior and language has not just on our life, but also, on other people's lives. This is true for how we behave on social media, as well as in the real world.

Creeps, Trolls and Other Dark Forces

A study published by the psychology journal, *Personality and Individual Differences*, found that around 5 percent of online users who self-identified as "trolls" had high scores of personality disorders, such as psychopathy, narcissism and Machiavellianism (also referred to as the "Dark Triad" in psychology). In case you are not up to speed on personality disorders, Machiavellianism describes a personality trait that leads an individual to manipulate and exploit others around them to achieve a personal goal. From an extensive piece in *Time* magazine exploring a timeline of how trolls have ruined the Internet, the writer states: "In 2011, trolls descended on Facebook memorial pages of recently deceased users to mock their deaths." Things have really intensified since then!

In 2012, after feminist Anita Sarkeesian started a Kickstarter campaign to fund a series of YouTube videos chronicling misogyny in video games, she received bomb threats at speaking engagements, doxing threats (researching and publicly broadcasting private information about a person), rape threats and an unwanted starring role in a video game called Beat Up Anita Sarkeesian. In June of 2020, Jonathan Weisman, the deputy editor of *The New York Times*, quit Twitter, on which he had nearly

35,000 followers, after a barrage of anti-Semitic messages. At the end of July, feminist writer Jessica Valenti said she was leaving social media after receiving a rape threat on Twitter against her daughter, who was five years old.

These examples of cyber-attacks are extreme, and it is heartbreaking to see how far certain individuals go to silence another human's voice who is trying to spread positivity and fight for a good cause. Greta Thunberg, the Swedish climate activist who has received much criticism and hate at a very young age, famously said, "When haters go after your looks and differences, it means they have nowhere left to go. And then you know you're winning!"

The Internet is beautiful, weird and fragile yet it can be mean and dangerous at the same time. It is an ecosystem that sometimes likes to laugh and other times, spreading fake news, exaggerates things before information has been revealed or stated.

Consider the case of 29-year-old vegan lifestyle star Yovana Mendoza Ayres, who built her platform on teaching 2.5 million subscribers how to live vegan and raw lifestyles. She had the food and skin care sectors locked down with years of meal plans, pictures and videos in her content anthology.

On a trip to Bali, according to *The Washington Post*, another YouTube star videoed Ayres eating fish at a restaurant. That small reel, those few minutes, put pressure on the woman's platform. Media worldwide picked it up. Viral. More like *viral venom*, in some cases. A dark force that did a great deal of damage.

The creator sent out an apology to her base, explaining that she had to eat more protein for medical reasons and was still trying to figure out her diet and lifestyle.

Eli Rosenberg from the *Washington Post* wrote: "The audience is not the only victim of the proliferation of false worlds online. Content creators suffer these algorithm-driven systems too, forcing them into a never-ending quest for viewers, ad money, sponsorships and engagement against dwindling attention spans."

The New Order of Connectedness

It surely doesn't sound so tempting to increase your online footprint after talking about what dark forces await out here. The problem is that they are waiting for us no matter what, if you just dip your toe in or you go all the way. The minute we start posting, we have possible exposure. It's inevitable. "Ignore them" would be the easiest advice to give, but if someone said something nasty, mean, and hurtful to you in real life, would you not respond? I bet you would. The difference is that online trolls are strangers you will hopefully never meet. They do not matter. Yet, comments that attack our identity, our body, or our general being are tough to ignore, particularly when the trolls are people we know. Classmates, friends of friends, or extended family members. I mentioned earlier that especially girls and young women are a frequent target for cyber-bullies.

There has to be early education on safer social media usage and that is specifically relevant for females that will be entering or planning to enter the workforce at some point and striving to go on the path to (senior) leadership. These young women have to rely on their confidence and self-belief to position themselves equally to their male counterparts and the reality is, the current social media landscape is significantly tilted against them.

The awareness of the concept of life-brand, maneuvering and embracing social media with purpose and intention, and feeling confident about displayed behavior and language, will ultimately lead young females not just to build early confidence through inspiring other young women to follow their lead, it'll slowly start to create a social media community that encourages women to feel more confident standing behind their purpose and identity.

With females being the most active on social media these days, there is a huge opportunity for young women to take their social media efforts to the next level by starting to build their life-brand through social media channels around something meaningful such as a hobby, a passion, an interest, expertise, or a cause they believe in rather than posting and sharing unintentional content that could potentially be damaging their future professional life. The core of this education focuses on how social media can be used in a safe(r) and controlled environment and how visibility and getting "likes and loves" can come from sharing purposeful content.

Social media used in a controlled way can actually lead to increased portrayed self-belief, a feeling of belonging to a community, and possibly feed the need to be liked, while at the same time powerfully position young women to successfully complete their education and enter the workforce displaying confident behavior right from the start. Purposefully and thoughtfully using social media can be a vehicle for young women to self-promote in a positive way, to build a strong life-brand around a meaningful personal interest and eventually their perceived purpose in life. Building a controlled life-brand guides women on the path to finding their true passion in life and helps them understand what legacy they wish to leave in the world, who they want to reach beyond their inner circles, and whose life they want to impact and change. It allows them to leave a legacy behind and make a long-lasting impact on the girls and soon-to-be young women of Generation Brand; the next wave of professional women they will eventually hire, promote, and guide on their paths to executive levels!

Confidence Hacks

Practice gratitude. A few times a week, take five minutes and think about all the things you are thankful for in your life. It makes you stay focused on the amazing things you have, over things—including likes and loves—you don't have.

IRINA SORIANO

4

Digital Destiny of the Sexes

"Where there is no struggle, there is no strength."

—Oprah Winfrey, American talk show host, television producer, actress, and author

So far, we've covered some insightful material about social media impact. Now, even though there has been some provocative talk about cancel culture and trolls, more controversial matters await as we take a slight pivot and look into women in the workplace, how we manage our careers compared to our male peers, and what impacts our choices and behaviors as it relates to business.

Research has shown that confidence, self-belief and comfort with self-promotion is significantly impacting how women at all levels maneuver their careers and are able to take risk as they advance their professional agenda. In this chapter, we will dive into why the early development of these traits is so critical to address some of the current challenges women are facing in the workplace.

Let's review what has been known for decades: there is the lack of gender parity in the workplace and an underrepresentation of females in leadership. Yearly reports detailing "Women in the Workplace" by reputable twin forces, McKinsey and Lean In, are conducted for good reason—progressive historical documentation, accountability and milestones. Two items stand out to from the 2019 edition: "Today, 44 percent of companies have three or more women in their C-suite, up from 29 percent of companies in 2015, totaling 21% of women in C-Suite positions," and recognition of the "broken rung", or a blind spot for the business world, which typically concentrates more on pipeline than progression. Broken rung at the step up to manager is the biggest obstacle that women face on the path to leadership, asserts the study. That initial missed promotion winds up holding women back for the rest of their careers. The same report published that 7 out of 10 women and 5 out of 10 men agree that men have an easier way to executive levels and that women have to work harder to show that they are worth being on top. It also stated that the public is "doubtful" that the US will ever reach the goal of full gender parity in politics or in the workplace.

With this problem generally being considered to be a true challenge, let's break it down into several issues that are contributing to the current state. McKinsey and Lean In have re-evaluated the term, *glass ceiling*, an "invisible, systemic barrier that prevents women from rising to senior leadership" and have shown that the problem to create a strong female pipeline begins much earlier; when women are facing the "broken rung" at the first-time promotion or being hired to manager. The broken rung significantly impacts the female pipeline in the workplace with only 72 women being promoted or hired to managers compared to 100 men accordingly as well as men holding 62% and women 38% of managerial positions. This phenomenon creates a thicker barrier for women to step over on the path to leadership early in their careers, lowering the numbers of females eventually reaching senior leadership. This same study discussed what companies need to do to positively impact the female pipeline by executing the following:

- Set a goal for getting more women into first-level management.

- Require diverse slates for hiring and promotions.

- Put evaluators through unconscious bias training.

- Establish clear evaluation criteria.

- Put more women in line for the step up to manager.

It's worth noting that the 2016 version of this same annual report by McKinsey & Company, "Women Matter", illustrated a significant shift from "line to staff jobs," meaning women move into supporting roles or subject matter expert positions rather than taking on the lead for large and complex projects as they approach senior leadership, while men continue at the same rate to progress to the top through line positions. Once women reach upper-middle management levels the shift has been so significant, that only 20% of females have profit and loss responsibilities.

Besides the lack of gender parity in leadership and managerial positions, we are also dealing with the problem of the gender pay gap. This challenge has been discussed, researched, and written about for decades and although the pay gap has slightly narrowed, women still only earned 85% of what men earned in 2018 in the US, Pew Research Center has announced, and what may be even more concerning is that based on these numbers, women needed to work an additional 39 days per year to equal their pay with male counterparts.

The title of another collection of stats online with an interactive tool by college major, "Why Women Can't Win", is both alarming and outrageous in 2021. Provided by Georgetown University's Center on Education and the Workforce, it states: "[…] men with bachelor's degrees make on average $26,000 more per year than women with the same credentials." **To all female readers:** Stop right now and think about what you would do with $26,000 additional income in your bank account. Envision how good that feels to see this extra amount reflected in your paycheck. Once you let that settle in, you realize what it feels like to do the same job as someone else and earn $26,000 less.

And all of these facts about the gender inequality and the pay gap were published during or prior to the year 2020. Unfortunately, the global pandemic has impacted the working environment for women even more and in ways we didn't even think possible. According to McKinsey and Lean In's latest "Women in the Workplace 2020" report, women and especially women of color have been impacted the most by the pandemic and "are more likely to have been laid off or furloughed during the Covid-19 crisis, stalling their careers and jeopardizing their financial security." The study also reveals:

- Women's workload between work and caring for children (and the household) has significantly intensified, having lost access to childcare and school.

- "Black women already face more barriers to advancement than most other employees [...] they're also coping with the disproportionate impact of Covid-19 on the Black community. And the emotional toll of repeated instances of racial violence falls heavily on them. The sad result is that '1 in 4 women are contemplating what many would have considered unthinkable less than a year ago: down-shifting their careers or leaving the workforce, as many as two million women.'"

Facing a Patriarchal Culture

A 2018 research paper discussing the "Patriarchal Culture's Influence on Women's Leadership Ascendancy" raises a few interesting findings centered on the obstacles women face while moving into leadership roles based on possible patriarchal culture in the workplace. One of the findings highlights that female, over male, mentors lead to mentored women being able to make their voices heard more in organizations with a female support system in place. Women supporting women on their career journeys have been shown to be a pivotal link in accelerating career advancement. The reality is that unless we get more women into leadership—quickly!—this issue will persist in the future. Life-brand comes into play here.

A female mentor will offer a less-experienced women wisdom, inspiration, and encouragement. This is usually done through sharing personal experience, challenges, and providing unique insights and perspective. Furthermore, a mentor will build up, bring positivity, instill confidence, and help the mentee to be their authentic self and the best version of themselves. In a 1-2-1 mentor/mentee relationship, goals would be discussed, and specific advice and mentorship will be provided. Considering the lack of female mentors in business, women in leadership and executive positions still do have the opportunity to influence, encourage, and inspire other young women from all over the world through the reach of their life-brand.

Life-brand will be a vehicle to provide young female professionals access to other businesswomen by learning from their experiences and insights. I am not saying this will replace direct 1-2-1 female mentorship per se; I am saying it will bring us closer to bringing more females to the top because we are enabling access to other established female professionals that are now indirectly "mentoring" other women in the workforce through the reach of their social media presence. We will cover this powerful opportunity in-depth when we dive into life-brand.

Another finding discussed in the mentioned study is that a patriarchal societal system promotes leadership in the workplace based on *typical* male characteristics. Women that felt they fit into the feminine stereotype were found to have less leadership aspirations for their future career, hence found gender stereotypes to be an obstacle to ambitious career aspirations. The study reinforces: "This issue is at the heart of socialization and how the patriarchal system has reinforced its values." Furthermore, "the patriarchal system is ingrained in society and affects the leadership style that women choose to adopt", with classic leadership competencies still being associated with male characteristics and attributes. "This male-dominated situation is a direct effect of the patriarchal system".

The situation might force female leaders to change their leadership style to adopt a more *male* approach, which creates unfair conditions for females at the top. Also, it forces women to choose—staying true to themselves risking their path to leadership or adopting male characteristics and behaviors to be perceived as *strong* and *capable*.

Having access to more aspiring female professionals and women at the top of organizations through the reach of their social media life-brands that fit into more male and feminine gender stereotypes will allow younger women to strive for their own authenticity as they are embarking on their path to management and executive levels. We know that women are up there that might fit more male or feminine gender stereotypes; however, the challenge becomes that not all young females are fortunate enough to have these female role models in their workplace and therefore lack access. A lack thereof results in a missed opportunity to develop strong self-belief in their own characteristics and have encouragement to be authentic and stay true to themselves. As we narrow the gender gap, enabling more females with different characteristics to be in leadership and executive roles will ultimately "contribute to a de-masculinization of leadership, not necessarily meaning a feminization of it, but loosening up management being culturally connected to men."

To highlight women facing patriarchic culture in the workplace further, the BBC conducted a survey based on the government's goal for women to make up at least a third of boards for the UK's 350 biggest companies by 2020, a target set by the Hampton-Alexander Review commissioned by the Department for Business, Energy, & Industrial Strategy (DBEIS). Fortunately, as of December 30, 2020, DBEIS announced that goal was achieved! It's still worth observing some of the reasons why women were lacking the board seats (listed in actual quote form):

- "I don't think women fit comfortably into the board environment."

- "There aren't that many women with the right credentials and depth of experience to sit on the board—the issues covered are extremely complex."

- "Most women don't want the hassle or pressure of sitting on a board."

- "Shareholders just aren't interested in the make-up of the board, so why should we be?"

- "All the 'good' women have already been snapped up."

- "We have one woman already on the board, so we are done—it is someone else's turn."

- "We need to build the pipeline from the bottom—there aren't enough senior women in this sector."

Interesting and shocking comments sounding like they were made in a previous century but coming from males at the top of UK's biggest companies, only highlights the issue of sponsorship for women from executive levels as these positions are dominated by men.

Sponsorship

We know there is a lack of female mentorship in the workplace due to a lack of women in senior positions. That being said, this does not mean women are generally under-mentored. Quite the opposite, according to *Harvard Business Review,* "women tend to be over mentored and under-sponsored." The key here is that while mentorship matters, the way to the top without having a sponsor is a steep one because there are distinct differences between mentorship and sponsorship. A mentor advises, encourages, inspires and helps to create a clear vision and goals for one's career. A mentor can also be in several positions of expertise as long as they can provide professional and personal development for their mentee. A sponsor, on the other hand, has to be a senior-level executive in the organization and will provide active support bringing a career vision to life. Furthermore, a sponsor will be able to provide important introductions to people in their network, will champion for who they sponsor, and most importantly...they are personally invested in their success.

I was very lucky. I had male sponsors throughout my career

that have taken personal interest in my growth and development and have provided me with career opportunities because they believed in my abilities and potential to add value to the organization.

I truly believe that the way to the top without a sponsor is incredibly hard, maybe even impossible. That is true for every professional. The issue with driving mentorship towards sponsorship lies in the commitment needed from the sponsor. True sponsorship with financial and time commitment is based on one's belief in the individual's potential, skills, and abilities and requires a relationship and understanding of those characteristics, hence cannot be mandated by anyone (while mentorship can be). A sponsor, unlike a mentor, has the true power to advance the individual's career and is not afraid to use it. With only 21% of women being in the C-Suite and women lacking access to male executives, thus lack of sponsorship, men are privileged with a much higher likelihood to be sponsored on their way to the C-Suite.

Confidence Reality Check

When looking at the gender pay gap, also reflected in the 2018 "Women Can't Win" report, women are less likely to choose high-paying occupations compared to their male peers. "For example, only 27 percent of chief executive officers, 44 percent of lawyers, and 43 percent of physicians and surgeons are women." This is not helping the issue at hand.

That being said, *Harvard Business Review* published a June 2018 piece illuminating that prior studies conducted on a lack of women asking for pay increases has been proven to be inaccurate, taking away from women actively contributing to the pay gap by *not asking* and fully putting the cause of the issue onto businesses. "Women who asked, obtained a raise 15% of the time, while men obtained a pay increase 20% of the time." Moreover, there was *no evidence* found that women are less likely to negotiate their salaries due to the fear of upsetting their bosses and actually ask for salary increases at the same rate as men. So, women ask, but men earn pay increases at a higher probability when asked for. The initial reaction here would probably be to blame this issue on the workplace.

What the study is not discussing is *how* women are asking for salary increases compared to their male peers, which for a change, is just as important as the *why* (sorry, Simon Sinek!). The question is, how are women asking for salary increases and how are they negotiating their salaries?

The what and the how are two completely different components and should be evaluated further (during my extensive research for this book, I did not come across any relevant studies that examined this question). Also, what is not being discussed is how quickly women abandon "asking" for pay increases compared to their male counterparts and how quickly they move on when the answer is "no" or not satisfying to them. It seems women have the confidence to "ask" but it can be assumed that there might be a lack of confidence to continue negotiation if the result does not seem acceptable yet. I have experienced numerous examples of young women seeking advice from me on how to negotiate deserved salaries, then they confidently asked for what they thought was justified, and still ended up taking the first offer because their initial ask for a higher pay was rejected. Thus, they immediately abandoned negotiation once and for all.

Touching on confidence, let's examine young women and their confidence to become leaders, as well as their general view on women in leadership. The study, "Leaning Out", conducted by Harvard University asserted, "teen girls who are key to closing the gender gap appear to face an age-old and powerful barrier: gender bias, and specifically biases about their leadership." The study shows that thousands of girls, boys, and adults hold persistent biases against girls as leaders. So, female confidence in leadership in teenagers, the next generation of professional women, is already significantly impacted by said biases. When surveyed who is perceived to be more effective in specific professions, 23% of girls and 40% of boys answered they preferred male over female leaders, and only 8% of girls said they actually prefer female leadership. Furthermore, the study examines how females feel about other females in power and there is clear bias; teenage girls tended not to support giving power to other girls in the context of student councils. Teenage girls presented with boy-led councils expressed higher average support for the council than when presented with girl-led councils.

Considering the problem with confidence in female leadership and the lack of support from teenage girls to their female peers shows a deeply rooted problem when it comes to women advocating for other women. It glaringly demonstrates that gender biases are driven from an early age, making the problem at hand culturally branded into women's perceptions about their female peers.

When looking at female confidence in general and the portrayal of such confidence through behavior, we are touching another part of the problem why women might not be in the position to drive gender parity themselves under the current circumstances.

A recent study, "Women and Self-Promotion: A Test of Three

Theories" published by SAGE, revealed that women in the workforce are actually no less self-confident in their skills and abilities than their male counterparts—they just don't *express* self-confidence through behavior by self-promotion to avoid social consequences, and to diminish the fear of not being liked or being perceived as "not nice". The same study shows that men can self-promote without having to display care or concern for others without being perceived negatively. They simply seem more self-confident in general.

The fear of self-promotion creates a significant barrier for women to advance their career and to portray their self-confidence in the workplace. Based on these facts, it seems that if women had a vehicle to self-promote while showing concern and care for others, the fear of social consequences and being perceived as "not nice", could be significantly diminished. This leads me back to the concept of life-brand. Controlling our life-brand, and actively developing it through social media channels while choosing a specific purpose in alignment with our identity, will allow for self-promotion while driving a purpose that ultimately helps, supports, influences, and impacts others in our social community and beyond.

The 2019 KPMG "Women's Leadership Study" exposed that 43% of businesswomen are less confident talking about accomplishments, which can probably be linked back to the discomfort of self-promotion. They also found that "extremely confident women are 22 [percent] more comfortable promoting themselves (compared to all businesswomen; 65% vs 43%). In addition, those that identified as extremely confident are 25 [percent] more comfortable asking for a new position." There clearly is something to be said about the connection between being comfortable to self-promote in the workplace and career advancement for women. According to the study, women harbor a fear of taking risks, which for 29% of all women, relates to confidence issues. "The findings indicate that increasing the confidence of individual employees benefits the organization as a whole, as those that said they were extremely confident were also more likely to take risks (small and large) and manage employees/staff." Finally, it is essential to recognize that it was also discovered that "women's self-confidence and openness to risk-taking appear to stem in part from experiences early in life. Self-confidence is a quality socialized as women grow up—with organized activities proving valuable in unlocking their confidence later in life."

If confident women are found to be more comfortable with self-promotion, and self-promotion is correlated to career success and risk taking, which help females to climb to the top quicker equal to their male counterparts, it is absolutely critical that we drive early confidence in the next wave of future professional women of Generation Brand. These efforts will position them strongly to be comfortable speaking about early accomplishments as they enter the workplace.

We just covered a lot of ground! Let's summarize what picture existing research, statistics, and data are painting for women in the workplace today:

- Women have to work harder to get to the top.

- Underrepresentation of women on manager levels are the true source for a lack of female leadership pipeline.

- Women lack sponsorship from (other female) executives.

- Women get paid significantly less than men.

- Women do not believe this situation is likely to change: "Men are more likely than women to say the U.S. will eventually reach gender parity in top political and corporate leadership positions." (*McKinsey and Lean In*)

- Women are asking for salary increases (note: they are less successful), yet it is not established with how much confidence they ask nor how easily they back down when they receive pushback.

- Women are less likely to choose higher paying occupations.

- Young teenage females have strong gender biases against female leaders.

- While women have self-confidence, they are less likely to portray it through self-promotion like their male peers due to fear of social consequences.

- There is a clear connection between confidence and self-promotion, as well as self-promotion and career advancement.

- Some women are risk-adverse due to a lack of confidence.

Light at the End of the Funnel

The good news in all of this insight and exposure is that we actually have seen some progress to create more favorable conditions for women to shape their career trajectory:

- "29.5 million women in the labor force have a bachelor's degree, effectively matching the number of college-educated men in the workforce. [...] Women now comprise 50.2% of the college-educated labor force, up from 45.1% in 2000." (*Pew Research Center*)

- "The traditional answer for women to overcome the pay advantages that men have traditionally held in the marketplace has been, and continues to be, more education.

And women have widely embraced this strategy." (*Georgetown University*)

- "A majority of Americans (59%) say there are too few women in top leadership positions in politics and in business today, with about half saying, ideally, there would be equal numbers of men and women." (*McKinsey and Lean In*)

Still, with progress over the past years, gender parity on leadership levels seems unattainable with women, and especially women of color, being underrepresented across all levels. While women in leadership and executive positions have the opportunity to use their life-brand to reach young professional females and make themselves accessible through social media, the next wave of professional women from Generation Brand will be the key to taking charge of their own destiny. Supported by strong efforts of companies and corporations, they hold the true power to facilitate change in gender parity and equality in the workplace.

Most of the time, the challenges women face in the workplace are probed from a specific perspective. This leads to suggestions and recommendations for businesses to do their part in closing the gender gap and to drive gender parity across all levels. There are two components to this challenge:

1. COMPANIES: have to make changes to foster gender parity in the workplace and create equal work environments for women, even more for women of color, and especially during and following COVID-19 that has and will continue to push a lot of females out of the workforce.

2. WOMEN: need to be enabled to build confidence early in life, so they can get more comfortable to self-promote and speak about their accomplishments, take more risks and actively drive their careers forward in less favorable conditions on the path to leadership. While they are doing so, women have the opportunity to create visibility in how they are successfully overcoming obstacles in business, which, in turn, will inspire and encourage other women, ultimately shaping a social media landscape of female role models for Generation Brand.

Don't get me wrong—there is absolutely no question that companies need to keep doing their part, and more, to actively contribute to closing the gender gap in the workplace. That alone will not be enough though. Women's fate cannot lie in the "companies' hands". Women themselves need to be the driver to create a paradigm shift towards gender equality in business, and it starts with their self-confidence enabling them to become more comfortable with self-promotion as they advance their careers and control their life-brands. When reading reports, books, or research on female lack of confidence, we often hear advice like the following (suggestions I was personally told in the past):

- Speak up.

- Get a seat at the table.

- Take risks.

- Create opportunities for yourself.

- Be aware of the impression you make.

- Go get it and ask for what you want.

The list goes on and on. I generally agree with all that is suggested. These things will not only make you look and sound more confident; they will eventually instill true confidence and self-belief. Some women and young females might naturally be more inclined to do these things; some might have made early experiences that helped them to be more confident and less afraid to go for it (that includes myself). But not everybody is that lucky. "Speak up" might be a life-long attempt of raising one's voice, if the person is an introvert, afraid of public speaking and has not been raised in an environment that encourages girls and young women to speak their mind. "You should", "you must", "you need". Advice that comes with a lack of actually teaching young girls and women *how* to build early confidence, *how* to be comfortable with self-promotion, and *how* to develop leadership skills at an early age; no matter what environment they grow up in.

The key to solve this challenge lies in driving confidence through self-promotion from an early age. Here, I refer to knowing and learning how to control one's life-brand. We know there is no comfort with self-promotion unless we find high levels of confidence in females. We know that the future females of Generation Brand are growing up surrounded by social media and can be exposed to severe confidence damage from an early age. This, in turn, will significantly diminish the chances for those young girls and women to develop comfort and self-belief standing behind their accomplishments.

The concept of life-brand, the awareness and education of it, the true understanding of its power and impact, as well as the endless influence just one woman's life-brand can have if fully controlled, will open the door of opportunity for the girls and young women of Generation Brand to close the gender gap for good.

Confidence Hacks

Give back. Make time for at least one person you know or do not know, to give back to them. Share experiences, advice, insight, network, or help them promote their life-brand.

5

The Power of Life-Brand

"When the whole world is silent, even one voice becomes powerful."

—Malala Yousafzai, Pakistani activist for female education, youngest Nobel Prize laureate

In marketing terms, a "brand" can be defined as a product and/or service name so it can take on an identity by itself. When we take the concept of brand out of marketing and into our personal lives, we refer to it as "personal branding", which can be defined as an intentional effort to shape a public perception by positioning yourself as an influence in a particular field, professional, and/or industry to stand out from your peers to gain credibility, as well as career advantages and to have a larger impact on your followership.

In the arena of this explicit marketing definition, the word, *brand*, is connected to the term, *identity*, for a product or service. It refers to a deliberately chosen identity that will be marketed to the public to increase sales, reach, and impact of said brand. For an individual, personal branding refers to an individual's public self-promotion efforts to drive personal goals and objectives such as career advancement or influence.

An iconic figure at the intersection of branding and marketing for decades, Rushion McDonald, oversees his own multimedia empire, 3815 Media, to show for it. He has a lot to say on the topic of personal branding—every day through various channels. I invited his take on branding in the lead-up to life-brand. He managed top entertainer Steve Harvey, 2000 until 2016, pre-Internet. (*Can you imagine?*) "Everything then was about having a fan club, and I still do by the way, because it is more authentic than a 'like' on social media. Fan clubs mean engagement and interaction. Twitter does not give you the demographics of someone typing in their name and other information that you can then research. Google has it. Facebook has it. Combine all these demographics that both have. If you are saying you are a brand, understand what it means. What do people care about? You need to find the people who care. Discover your brand relationship with those people. Short term means media engagement. Long term means brand."

This is great foundational information, since the concept of life-brand goes beyond the concept of personal branding and brings different components together.

It identifies one person as distinct from others and is defined by the person's unique **purpose** and **identity** through their everyday displayed public behavior and chosen language in the real and virtual world, shaping the public's perception about the life-brand owner.

This concept expands the definition of personal branding as an intentional effort of using your purpose in life to impact change, to build (early) confidence and be comfortable with self-promotion (I am particularly addressing my female readers with the latter). Life-brand takes into account your public display of (un) intentional language and behavior (aka how you portray your identity to others). While personal branding is clearly defined as *intentional* efforts to advance your career and increase influence, life-brand develops itself *with* or *without* your control, *with* or *without* your intention. Like personal branding, life-brand can positively influence your development and career, if understood and controlled, or, if unaware of its power or existence, it can negatively impact your (future) career, family, and aspirations by virtue of disadvantageous public perception of you.

Considering this additional component of life-brand, you might be perceived by the public in an inaccurate way based on interpretation of your unintentional behavior or language that might not be reflecting your true identity. Rushion says that we are in a historic time of unabashed fertile ground for recognizing that first, we all possess a life-brand and, secondly, understanding the fundamentals of enrollment and engagement is imperative for grasping control over simply connectedness between tools.

"Those that make your life better or make you feel better about your authentic self are the motivational people and brands that have the staying power online. Entertainers, actors. Then you have the fear followers. Who do you want to *be* or follow? Fear drives a lot of engagement and enrollment and people trying to understand who they are, and they are susceptible to misinformation. I don't ever want to be a person who walks out in public and gets stared at like I am lesser than what I have become or am capable of becoming. An element of my brand is as an African

American man. I had to couch that before George Floyd. After George Floyd, people are more accepting and allowed my talent to shine as a black man, a person of color, a gay person, and so that is really a good thing. We should always be accepting of who people are and what we can do in making them more comfortable. It creates a more competitive environment and we're all tax-paying customers. Branding and humanity 101 first. Build your life-brand and build respect."

I think brand and respect definitely go hand in hand. Self-respect and respect for others playing in the same cyberspace, workspace, living space.

Branding can also be defined as being *marked with a branding iron*. In the context of life-brand, we can relate this definition to a person's identity as being branded for life, meaning no matter what efforts are undertaken, the "mark" may fade, but the damage will likely remain forever. Controlling your life-brand from an early age will not just protect against possible missteps, but furthermore allow you to define a true identity, the "real you", which will, without a doubt, lead you to eventually finding your purpose in life.

Controlled Life-Brand

A controlled life-brand (Figure 1) will be defined consisting of two components: your *identity* and your chosen *purpose* in life. *Identity* in the context of life-brand is defined as the summary of your behavior and language displayed through social media or in the real world, while *purpose* can be discovered through the vehicle of a passion, an idea, your profession or expertise in a certain field, and an interest or hobby you pursue.

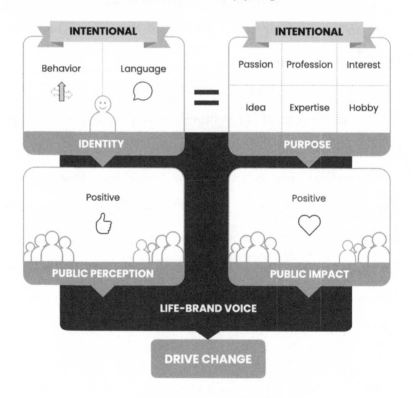

Figure 1. Controlled Life-Brand

Managing the combination of and connection between identity and purpose is crucial to truly controlling a life-brand rather
than being controlled by it. This means your behavior and language have to be in alignment with your chosen purpose and
need to be portrayed with integrity. That is the case for social
media, as well as behavior and language displayed in the real
world (because a public temper tantrum can also make its way
onto the Internet). Sharing your purpose with the world through
social media channels is an intentional, controlled effort you un-
dertake. Make no mistake, it is not random.

Public display of purpose can lead to significant positive impact on others and your community, thanks to the vast reach social media channels have these days. When life-brand is owned
and controlled, it is created by both public perception and positive impact and becomes a powerful vehicle to impact, reach,
and influence others. When the concept of life-brand is understood, controlled and proactively developed with integrity between purpose and identity, the concept enables you to establish
a unique life-brand voice powerfully influencing others who lis-
ten and inspire them to take action in response.

Purpose

When people hear the word, *purpose*, they often connect it to a humongous goal or a legacy they leave behind when they leave this earth. A purpose is usually seen as a life-long journey that is intended to change people's lives and to drive change. When we speak about purpose in the context of a controlled life-brand, it can, of course, be just that: accomplish big things and change the world. For many, a purpose is related to a special gift, such as a doctor curing a disease that affects many people, or an athlete who becomes the best in their field worldwide and a role model for many wanting to follow their journey. But not everybody has this kind of aspiration. No matter what your aspiration or special gift, you can easily have a purpose in life and use it to control your life-brand.

Your life-brand can only be fully controlled if you have picked a specific purpose. If I examine my own life-brand, my initial purpose was my profession. Over time, my passion of making an impact on closing the gender gap has become another purpose my life-brand is centered around; it is an *and*, not an *or*. If I flash back to when I was a teenager and young woman, my chosen purpose would have certainly not been aligned to any of these things. I did not have the same level of professional experience, and the gender gap was not top of mind.

Your purpose will evolve and change over the course of a lifetime and so it should, people grow up and evolve. So will your purpose. To make it easier to find a purpose you can build your current life-brand on, let's look at the following:

- **Passion:** My passion is making a contribution to closing the gender gap and being a role model for girls and young women to control their life-brand to build strong confidence early in life so they can take control of their careers and feel equal to their male counterparts. But a passion could also be to save an animal species, for example. Our friend's 19-year-old daughter, who is studying animal sciences and wants to be a conservationist, has made it her passion to change legal regulations for pangolins, the world's most trafficked mammal, to protect these beautiful creatures.

- **Idea:** An idea can tackle a problem, a challenge or, improve a situation or circumstance. It could be an invention. It could be a creative thought that no one else had before. Building a purpose around an idea leaves room for endless opportunity.

- **Profession:** If you build your purpose around your profession, it requires you to actually have experience in said profession in some shape or form.

- **Expertise:** Expertise as a purpose can be connected to your profession, the industry or business you work in. But expertise can be much more than that. Anybody can become an expert in a particular field, that includes teenagers and young adults. If you have invested time to study and research particular topics of interest and feel your expertise is worth building a purpose around, I would encourage you to do so!

- **Interest:** Interests are easy and great to use as a purpose for your life-brand. Having an interest does not mean you should have expertise or deep knowledge, as maybe you are in the middle of becoming an expert! If you have an interest in baking, yet are not very good at it, you might center your purpose around developing your baking skills and share your journey with your social media followers.

- **Hobby:** Are you playing a sport? Maybe an instrument? Hobbies are a great purpose.

Not every purpose has the potential to change the world (although some will)—and that is not the goal! Picking one and aligning your social media presence around it, and posting content that is connected to it, should be the ultimate aim. Being aligned to your purpose at all times will give you the power to build a followership that can identify with it through one or various social media channels, and most importantly, it still gives you the ability to get "likes and loves", make new connections, and build a social media network.

Purpose should set you apart from others, yes, but it should also connect you to others so they can identify with your purpose and help you drive change amongst your friends and family, in your community, your city, your state, country, and yes, maybe even in the world. A purpose should never be brought to life by one person only, it needs followership and support from others. It should be an inspiration to others that can identify with it and that may have struggled to find one on their own. Purpose is supposed to be shared; it should create a community. It is supposed to spread positivity.

I recently chatted with a young woman who said, "If I build my life-brand and purpose around my hobby of playing the guitar, can I ever post a photo of my dog again?" Of course, you can!

Posting about your life is fun and can totally be part of your life-brand. I share photos about my dog and my husband and I being out in New York all the time. As long as what you post is not in misalignment with your identity you are good to go. Think about it this way: if you build your life-brand around your hobby of playing a sport, posting a photo of you vomiting on your friend's front lawn after a night out is probably a bad idea.

Identity

Your identity is shaped by two components, your *behavior* and *language*.

Behavior

Behavior can be portrayed publicly, privately when surrounded by few people or one other person, or without anybody witnessing at all. Life-brand is shaped by behavior in two ways. Your behavior has at least one witness, the observer being affected by your behavior or not (can be observed from afar). Behavior in this context is defined as your physical actions. Those can either be captured by someone on a phone and shared on social media with or without your consent or the observer is making a statement about your behavior publicly without direct evidence.

Behavior can also be defined as actions you portray and capture yourself and then voluntarily share with the public through various social media channels.

If behavior is captured by you or another person, it'll likely be in the form of video or photo recording your action. I consider this behavior unintentional. That can totally be fine, but in certain cases there is a significant chance that your behavior is in misalignment with your purpose, hence it might create a negative public perception of your identity (that means people now have a perception of you that you really do not identify with).

If you understand the concept of a controlled life-brand and you realize that any action filmed or taken on a picture (ever!) is part of your life-brand, you will start acting in a way that has integrity with your chosen purpose (or at least if you decide not to control your life-brand and pick a purpose, you won't screw up your future). To make it even clearer what unintentional captured behavior can do to your life-brand, let's look at the example of American singer Ariana Grande. In 2015, she was filmed licking doughnuts in a store in Los Angeles, US. The video was shared on social media and received millions of views.

In the clip, the 22-year-old Grande was seen to touch doughnuts with her tongue while laughing and saying, "What the fuck is that? I hate Americans. I hate America." She issued an apology, as reported by CNN, saying, "Seeing a video of yourself behaving poorly, that you have no idea was taken, is such a rude awakening, that you don't know what to do. I was so disgusted with myself." Grande's purpose is built around her music and connection to her fans, so this unintentional display of inappropriate behavior was in complete misalignment with said purpose. Luckily, Grande was able to correct her misstep, owned up to it, and turned the corner (yes, she was forgiven licking those donuts).

Language

Language is defined as spoken and written words. It can be captured as an audio recording, through video or screenshots or copies of written statements. Language can create a strong public reaction when captured on video/audio, but also impacts public perception significantly if surfaced in the form of a social media post or comment you make online. A public example of displayed language that has received extreme backlash and cancelled a career is a controversial tweet from the actress Rosanne Barr about longtime Barack Obama aid Valerie Jarrett saying, "Muslim brotherhood & planet of the apes had a baby." ABC quickly announced they were dropping Barr's reboot show "Rosanne" after the racist and Islamophobic tweet was posted. But it did not end there. Instead of owning up to what was spoken publicly, Barr blamed her post on the sleeping pill Ambien, which led to a Twitter response from the drug manufacturer saying "People of all races, religions and nationalities work at Sanofi every day to improve the lives of people around the world. [...] While all pharmaceutical treatments have side effects, racism is not a known side effect of any Sanofi medication."

Acting and Speaking with Intention

When it comes to controlling your life-brand, *intention* ties it all together. Intention means to act and speak in a way that you have thoughtfully chosen, being aware of the weight your words and actions have on others and possibly yourself; the consequences that follow actions and words.

Intention is critical to controlling your life-brand, because it trains your mind to actually reflect on what you put on social media, be it in your public or private accounts. I am sure a lot of us have woken up one morning and were not too happy with what we posted on Twitter, Facebook or Instagram when we looked at it with a sober pair of eyes. DELETE! The problem is that as much as you hit the delete button, the cloud never forgets what you shared. By the time you make up your mind about that post or photo, someone else might have already shared it to a broader and public audience.

When controlling your life-brand, your act and your speech is intentional. That goes beyond posting on social media with intention; it also reflects what we do in the real world due to constant visibility. These days, we have to assume that everything we say and do outside of being alone might make it onto social media and therefore, becomes a vital piece of our life-brand.

When I first reflected on the concept of life-brand and living in integrity with my purpose and my identity, meaning creating an intentional life for myself, it was an eye opener how many times I have just hit the "post" button, snapped a photo of someone or made a video without giving it a second thought. Posting about others, even if it's supposed to be funny, a joke, something silly (I know, we have all been there), should come with the immediate thought of, *what is my intention sharing this photo or video on social?* If there isn't any, don't post it. Do not make a contribution to someone's life-brand unless you have a clear intention in doing so. Think of it as a really bad tattoo. You can cover it up, you can even try to laser it off, but you can never erase it.

When it comes to controlling your own life-brand and protecting others' life-brands that are in your inner circle, I would always ask the following questions before you hit the "post" button:

- Would I like this photo/video to be associated with my own life-brand?

- Is this photo/video representative of my, or of the other person's true identity?

- Could this post harm me or the other person?

- Could this photo/video impact my or the other person's future employment if leaked? (Everything can be leaked these days.)

Someone said to me the other day when I spoke about intention in regard to life-brand, that she thinks it's too much effort and too much work to always be intentional; that sometimes we just "share" without any meaning. I found it interesting that she linked intention to effort. I explained that it simply means to have awareness of what you are saying and doing and to be clear why you share content with the world. Intention does not mean every post needs to specifically support our purpose and have deep meaning. It means to only share what is aligned to our identity, who we really are and how we wish to be perceived by the world.

I post photos of my dog with the intention of sharing how cute he is. It's not meaningful, but it is also not misaligned to my identity or my life-brand purpose of enabling women to close the gender gap in the workplace.

We have talked about criticism, trolls and other dark forces. I am not saying these won't come your way, as even if you build your life-brand with 100% intention, they will find you eventually. But think about how much easier it is to ignore them, when all you have shared on social media was intentional, thought-through, and you are fully standing behind it? It's a much different situation than receiving backlash on something you are not proud of (ala Roseanne Barr). Intention will also protect you from others recording and sharing content of you that could possibly mark your life-brand for good and attract hundreds of thousands of comments because you will start acting and speaking with intention around others in the real world.

Building a controlled and intentional life-brand with an aligned purpose and identity allows you to not just actively impact your direct social media community, but also, to inspire others to follow your lead and support your chosen purpose. More and more people controlling their life-brand will do several things over time:

1. It will slowly shift the social media landscape towards a community of powerful life-brand role models. Especially girls and women of all ages will be able to grow up in a social media world of encouragement, self-love and promotion, as well as positivity.

2. It will motivate others to go on the journey to find their own purpose.

3. It will build early confidence in teenagers and young

adults, especially females, that stand behind their chosen purpose and who understand the consequences of posting content on social media that is unintentional or misaligned with their identity.

4. It will make people think twice before hitting the "post" button or taking a photo/video of someone (or themselves) displaying behavior or language that does not represent their or the other's identity.

Developing a Leader's Life-Brand Voice

"Brand voice" in the context of marketing refers to an alignment in the selection of words and brand value when reaching the brand's audience. It describes how a brand delivers its personality to the target audience. Life-brand voice acts in a similar way; it is defined through the uniformity between your purpose and your identity displayed through behavior and language. If uniform, it conveys your powerful life-brand to the world through its voice, possibly reaching a vast audience through various social media channels. A life-brand voice can only be achieved with a fully controlled life-brand. It is a powerful vehicle to impact change in your surroundings, community, workplace, industry...and beyond. When you fully understand your long-term purpose (and this is supposed to be a fun discovery), you align your identity to that purpose, you drive positive impact and create a positive public perception of your life-brand, your life-brand voice will start to reach many people that might possibly support your purpose and help you drive change. Your life-brand voice can only be developed thanks to a very important medium: social media. In order to develop a strong life-brand voice, having access to 3.8 billion smart phone users, is crucial. Reach is key.

Relating back to closing the gender gap we discussed earlier in this book, the outcome of women raising their life-brand voices as a joint force will drive a paradigm shift, a quantum leap in gender equality in the workplace. Women actively controlling their life-brands and developing clear life-brand voices through social media, demonstrating their comfort with self-promotion, their leadership, and their self-belief and confidence, will change the current social media landscape for girls and future young women of Generation Brand. They will turn it into a beacon of hope, inspiration, and motivation to also control their life-brands from an early age. Generation Brand will be fueled by confidence, courage to self-promote, as well as deep self-belief in their own abilities and strengths, thanks to the reach of other people's life-brand voices.

A strong life-brand voice example: Greta Thunberg

An example of a life-brand owner with immense community impact is Greta Thunberg, a young Swedish environmental activist who established a strong life-brand voice at an early age by creating awareness about climate change and a possible existential crisis for humanity arising from it. Thunberg has been thinking about climate change—and the lack of action to curb it—since age 8. She has said she didn't understand why adults weren't working to mitigate its effects.

Thunberg is known for her strong social media presence using platforms such as Instagram to promote her purpose, motivating other young females to follow her lead to promote other activist causes.

We saw huge support for her purpose, her identity and the positive impact she is having on the world. For example, in March 2019, Thunberg led more than 1 million students around the world as they walked out of Friday classes to protest inaction on climate change. *Time* magazine named her the "2019 Person of the Year". She was my person of the year, too!

The other side to her public life-brand were comments about her Asperger's, her being too young to contribute to political discussions, her choice of words in public settings, conspiracy theories she was collaborating with the terrorist organization ISIS and much more. Facing such backlash has only fueled her to drive her cause, bring others with her and to stay true to her purpose and identity when reacting or ignoring such comments and criticism.

In January 2021, she turned 18. On Instagram, she has 10.5 million followers. On Twitter, she has 4.2 million. What will her life-brand reflect in ten years?

Life-Brand for Young Professional Women

To all of the young female professionals reading this book, let's be clear. You have the same capabilities as your male counterparts. You may just not be expressing it! And if you aren't expressing yourself, others will not know the true you, your potential, and your abilities. This thought of "not being enough" didn't arise out of nowhere. If you're thinking it today, even as circumstances around you like your title, best group of gal pals, achievements and accolades say differently, these thoughts can be reversed. This predicament can be reversed.

The "Women and Self-Promotion" study referenced earlier, revealing women's fear of self-promotion as a result of social consequences, defined those consequences as "women's self-promotion is limited by fear that others will derogate them for bragging about their accomplishments as is suggested by backlash avoidance theory." It can also be assumed that self-promotion through branding can be seen as portraying a big ego, being "full of themselves" or have over-the-top self-belief which could deflect on some women's need to be perceived as "nice" and to be "liked". This theory is supported by a finding that "women perceive their own promotion to be limited when it is identifiable, but they can self-promote more effectively when they do so under a feminine pseudonym." It is interesting to learn that women do not seem to have any fears around self-promoting if the accomplishment and success cannot be directly related back to them.

The fear of and the lack of investment in self-promotion to avoid social consequences in the real and virtual world ultimately contributes to women not being well-positioned to face the broken rung due to a general lack of displayed confidence, which we referred to earlier, and what is defined by McKinsey and Lean In as the biggest obstacle for women to progress to senior leadership and the C-Suite at first-time promotion to manager. The ultimate consequence of this is that not enough women progress to manager level and go down the path to leadership, and we now have 62% of manager-level positions being held by men.

By women not being aware of the potential negative impact

they might have on the gender gap in the workplace by shying away from self-promotion, they are actually widening that gap even more by not being a great role model for girls and future young women of Generation Brand. With women from 18-29 years old being the most active on social media, there is a missed opportunity to engage with the soon to be young women of Generation Brand to portray what positive influence self-promotion and life-brand building through social media can have when used in a controlled and safe environment on women's portrayal of confident behavior.

The "shine theory" developed by Ann Friedman and Aminatou Sow refers to "a practice of mutual investment with the simple premise that 'I don't shine if you don't shine.'" It particularly relates to women making a commitment to collaborate rather than compete with each other. And this is what life-brand is all about!

It has the power to change today's social media ecosystem by giving young girls the belief in other women's leadership capabilities as well as their own, creating visibility into struggles others have as they climb their career ladder to the top and how they encounter them. Most importantly, it will inspire girls and young women all over the world that gender equality in the workplace will happen if they follow other women's lead and start controlling their life-brands from an early age to build bullet-proof confidence.

Confidence Hacks

Reflect on your accomplishments. Rather than constantly looking forward, make time to look backwards to reflect on all the great things you accomplished, small and large.

6

Life-Brand Awareness

"It is sometimes the most fragile things that have the power to endure and become sources of strength."

—May Sarton, Belgian-American poet, novelist and memoirist

My parents used to collect antiques when I was a child. A lot of them! I remember my mother showing me a glued (very expensive) plate when I was older, telling me that I had broken it as a toddler. I had a tendency to pull down tablecloths, so my parent's plates and valuable decanters eventually made it into a vitrine, out of my vicious little hands right to safety. While you could hardly tell that my mother had glued the plate back together, the cracks always remained and gave it a little "edge".

The plate I broke represents our life-brands in many ways. Plates are fragile and break easily, and so do our life-brands. The glue made it look almost unharmed, but the cracks remain until this day.

A life-brand can be incredibly strong especially when built and controlled over the course of a life-time; tightly aligned with our identity. That being said, just like the plate, a life-brand is also incredibly fragile, if the connection between purpose and identity is not understood and respected.

I obviously broke that plate unintentionally without thinking of the consequences. "Breaking" our life-brand can happen the same way; one misstep of unintentional behavior or language in misalignment with our purpose and identity can lead to a per-manent break. It might even brand us for life. We can, of course, glue it back together, but it is important to understand that the "cracks" in our life-brand will always remain visible in the cloud.

If life-brand is "glued" back together, we are speaking of a life-rebrand. While missteps will still be visible and some public perception and opinion might remain, we have the opportunity to re-establish our life-brand, follow the same purpose or choose a new one, and realign our identity. Public perception can be impacted and changed over time, allowing us to regain our life-brand voice.

Misaligned Life-Brand

Carrying a misaligned life-brand (Figure 2) means that we have chosen a purpose and have actively built our life-brand around said purpose.

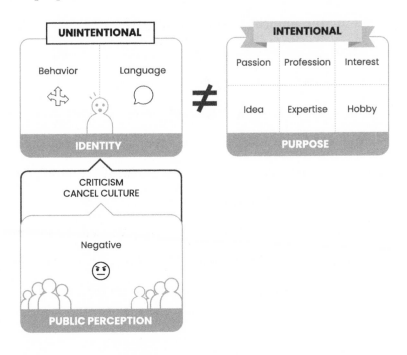

Figure 2. Misaligned Life-Brand

What is missing in this scenario is the awareness that life-brand is more than just purpose; it is also shaped by our identity portrayed through behavior and language that, if not intentional, can harm our life-brand purpose significantly.

So, even if our purpose is intentional, the unintentional display of misaligned identity will overpower your purpose with negative public perception and can lead to criticism or even cancel culture. It can instantly silence our life-brand voice.

Identity through unintentional display of behavior and language will instantly overpower our purpose, even if it was built and established for years resulting in a powerful and positive life-brand. The immediate effect of negative public perception through social media will heavily impact our life-brand and instantly "rebrand" us in a possibly negative fashion. As the life-brand owner, you have the possibility to re-establish your purpose and align your identity in the event of misalignment, but you might always be faced with the permanent "branding" as a result from this misalignment.

A damaged life-brand, or worse, being "cancelled", does not mean it cannot be repaired and gained control of again. Let's visit a couple of famous examples of misaligned life-rebrands.

Tiger Woods

A shining example of a re-established life-brand after being "cancelled" is Tiger Woods, the American professional golfer. Woods is regarded as one of the greatest golfers of all times and centered his life-brand around the sport and his accomplishments. In 2010, Wood's career was shadowed by a series of major challenges involving injuries, a DUI arrest, and a cheating scandal of significant proportion eventually leading to the divorce from his wife and major sponsors dropping him. In order to rebuild his life-brand, Woods issued a detailed public apology on *CNN* saying, "I was unfaithful. I had affairs. I cheated", "For all that I have done, I am so sorry" and "The same boundaries that apply to everyone apply to me."

Woods built his life-brand around the purpose of the sport through his passion and expertise. The public perception of Woods was extremely positive. Through his unintentional behavior and through others going public without his consent to highlight him being unfaithful to his wife, there was a clear misalignment between the identity he portrayed and his purpose. The newly perceived identity now overpowered his established life-brand and led to a significant negative public perception and partly cancel culture with him losing some of his sponsorships.

The public apology and a major golf comeback enabled Woods to realign his purpose and identity, while his missteps will always remain public and forever accessible to the world.

Jimmy Fallon

Mid-2020, Jimmy Fallon received serious backlash over a surfaced video from the year 2000 of him doing a blackface impression of Chris Rock on Saturday Night Live. Rock himself took the surfaced video lightly stating to the *New York Times*, "Hey, man, I'm friends with Jimmy. Jimmy's a great guy [...] And he didn't mean anything. A lot of people want to say intention doesn't matter, but it does. And I don't think Jimmy Fallon intended to hurt me. And he didn't." Fallon owned up to what happened and issued a public apology on his show, saying, "And I had to really examine myself, really examine myself in the mirror this week, because a story came out about me on *SNL* doing an impression of Chris Rock in blackface. And I was horrified. Not of the fact that people were trying to cancel me or cancel the show, which was scary enough. But the thing that haunted me the most was, how do I say, 'I love this person, I respect this guy more than I respect most humans, I am not a racist, I don't feel this way?'"

Mistakes do happen. We might say or do things we are not

proud of or that we regret later in life when the context changes. Back in the day, mistakes might have happened when nobody was filming or listening, but due to a death of privacy and constant visibility, displaying public language and behavior now have a high likelihood of being documented and stored in the cloud for the years to come. The awareness and education of life-brand and understanding how we can control it will significantly shape the young men and women of Generation Brand on how life-altering mistakes can be avoided or if occurred, be accepted, owned, and used to teach others around us not to repeat them.

Uncontrolled Life-Brand

An uncontrolled life-brand (Figure 3) shapes itself solely based on our unintentional behavior or language and there is no chosen purpose to guide our life-brand. In this scenario, life-brand literally has a life on its own!

Uncontrolled life-brand happens when there is a lack of awareness and education on this concept, so you might currently fall into this category (that's okay, I was there until a few years ago).

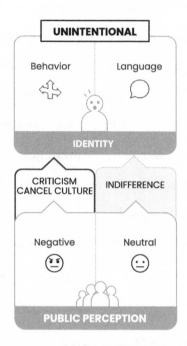

Figure 3. Uncontrolled Life-Brand

In this scenario, social media content might be shared by you or by others without your consent, all of it unintentional. Generally speaking, a lot of people never encounter any issues living a life with an uncontrolled life-brand. I, in fact, know many people that are totally happy to do so (my husband is one of them). But not actively controlling your life-brand does not mean to ignore the concept—you should still understand what possible life-brand ignorance consequences are.

Uncontrolled life-brand, if not understood, can lead to two

possible outcomes. The first is that negative public perception can be shaped based on your unintentional behavior or language shared on social media, which ultimately leads to your life-brand taking shape without your control. The Brisbane, Australia, Poo jogger Andrew Douglas Macintosh (64 years of age) is an example of an uncontrolled life-brand. His behavior publicized on social media cost him his employment after having to resign. Macintosh was caught right in the act defecating on people's properties during his morning run on several occasions. The picture of him, his pants down, holding a piece of toilet paper, made it around the world.

The other option is that no public perception is created at all. Nothing happens. An example could be that you are only sharing holiday and dog snaps, communicate with friends and family through social channels, and you generally do not post anything controversial, daring, or provocative. This also means that you never happen to do anything others might deem inappropriate or social media share-worthy. In this case, you will probably have an uncontrolled and infamous life-brand. "That's fine by me," you might say. And I agree. Not everybody in the world will tout the interest to actively control their life-brand and find their purpose. But there is something to be said about protecting yourself to be controlled by your own life-brand—so, at least be aware.

A recent example of an uncontrolled life-brand with an unintentionally displayed behavior is Liberty University's president, one of the world's largest evangelical Christian colleges, Jerry Falwell Jr. While students at the university are told "to dress modestly" and are "banned from consuming media that feature nudity or sexual content", he posted a picture on his personal social media channel of him and a young unknown female, his pants unzipped and midriff out, while holding a glass of dark liquid he captioned as "black water". While apparently, the photo was shot "all in good fun", Mr Farewell has taken a leave of absence after "the image provoked outrage and charges of hypocrisy from the political right and left, with Republican lawmaker Mark Waller, chairman of the powerful House Republican Caucus, calling on Mr Falwell to step down" according to the *BBC*.

From Awareness to Execution

When life-brand, its reach, impact and possible consequences are thoroughly understood and it is controlled and shaped in an intentional way, the challenge we see with social media impact on Millennials, Gen Z, and Generation Brand turns into a huge opportunity. Social media can become a powerful tool to control your life-brand and to build a strong life-brand voice that can benefit from an even broader, maybe even global, "audience reach". Intentionally using your passion, interest, expertise etc. to slowly walk down the path of discovering your true purpose in life can, of course, be done in the real world, but is even more impactful if driven virtually through social media channels based on the vast reach and impact life-brand voice can have through these channels. Portraying your purpose through social media can take various shapes depending where you are in your life-brand journey. A few options, especially for people that are in early life-brand stages, are the following:

Pictures and videos

A perfect way to speak about your life-brand purpose on social media is to share pictures and videos that truly represent you and your identity. Those could feature you, people in your life that wish to be associated with your purpose, or other people that you admire and are inspired by. This is an effective way to be intentional about who you are and to be aware of how you act and speak while broadcasting yourself to the world. As mentioned earlier, you can still post things that are not directly related to your chosen purpose as long as they are still in alignment with your true identity (being careful not to perpetuate a misaligned life-brand!). I love to post pictures and videos about my passion-purpose, because I find it's a fantastic way to reach girls and young women, spread positivity, help build confidence, and encourage them to go for what they want in life. Also, it is a wonderful vehicle to allow people in your community to truly know you, your character, and what you stand for.

Comments, likes, loves and re-shares

Commenting, liking, loving, clapping (depending on your favorite social media channel) is a wonderful way to not just build your own life-brand, but also, to lift others up around you that decided to do the same. It is a marvelous way to "give back" and allow others to know why they inspire you and why you decided to take two minutes out of your day to comment on a post they shared. An even greater way to build your own life-brand while supporting theirs is to share their posts on your own platform. Think how wonderful it feels if someone takes the time to share one of your posts with their followers because they felt encouraged and inspired by what you said or did.

Articles and blogs

Some of us are prolific writers and prefer to share thoughts in writing rather than through video. A simple way to positively contribute to your life-brand is to either start a blog or to write articles. I started my professional life-brand through writing articles about the tactics of my job because it took me a little longer to get comfortable being on video. Your blog posts or articles can be featured through your social media channels as an efficient source of content to share with your followers.

Webinars and podcasts

This part probably speaks more to the advanced life-brand owners amongst us. Once your life-brand voice captures more attention, you might have the opportunity to be invited to webinars and podcasts and to either speak or be interviewed about your purpose. It is a fantastic way to reach a vast audience, to drive change, and to share your purpose with others in the world. Don't be too impatient; you will eventually get there if you haven't already had the opportunity to participate. You can, of course, share any webinar and podcast appearances through your social channels, but usually the organizer will do the same for you, which can be very powerful.

Trend is Your Friend

One thing is clear: Social media is here to stay. It is increasingly gaining more influence on our lives, and using it purposefully and with intention to shape and control our life-brands is extremely powerful. It has become a vital part of people's lives; therefore, it is even more important to embrace this culture and to use its power to drive positive impact and change.

Going back to the original problem of social media misuse, we highlighted the dominant social media use of young females (18- to 29-year-olds). The chase for "likes and loves" and acceptance of virtual communities, the need to gain popularity, and using social media to compare themselves to their peers, has increasingly become popular driving more and more young women to post daring, unseen, questionable and provoking content that, in some instances, led to significant negative public perception and even cancel culture.

We also highlighted that there was a lack of understanding the impact that portraying certain behavior and language on social media has on someone's education, career and future life.

The concept of life-brand and controlling and shaping said life-brand through social media addresses these challenges. Only sharing intentional content through social media with integrity and a specific purpose, allows young females to gain the exact same satisfaction they might be chasing: getting "likes", being accepted by social communities, portraying their identity and purpose publicly to gain attention, while at the same time, being able to compare their own efforts to others in their social media circles. In this scenario, the difference is that social media, its impact, and reach is fully understood, and young females know how to harness this powerful vehicle to gain visibility through positivity and purpose. Furthermore, understanding social media, as well as its benefits and pitfalls, will enable young females to be more cautious about their chosen language and behavior outside of social media, removing the risk to be filmed, photographed, or recorded while using unintentional and possibly socially unacceptable language or behavior.

Confidence Hacks

Don't take yourself too seriously. Have the confidence to laugh at yourself when you screw up or things don't go as planned. Having a light attitude when mistakes happen helps to see them as confidence boosters and learning moments rather than setbacks.

IRINA SORIANO

7

Life-Brand Skills

"The key to successful leadership today is influence, not authority."

—Ken Blanchard, American author

When you choose to contribute to the public conversation through social media aligned with your purpose, you are stepping into the life-brand "arena". Being in the "arena", which is defined as "speaking up and daring to effect change" by Brené Brown, an American professor/lecturer and author, will teach you various life and leadership skills and allows you to develop traits and characteristics that we usually only gain as we advance in life and in our careers.

Controlling your life-brand and living with integrity and alignment to your identity at all times requires a lot of courage and self-awareness. Once you are actively controlling and building your life-brand with the goal of driving positive impact and building a positive public perception of yourself (and yes ladies, I am talking about self-promotion with a purpose), there is always a risk that you will face other individuals that are in disagreement with your purpose or your identity and therefore, decide to challenge you in a public setting by commenting on your social media posts. You might call them haters, dark forces, or trolls...the results are the same, they will bring you criticism and backlash. Being publicly challenged and standing behind your intentional purpose and identity requires self-confidence in your life-brand and its purpose. Most importantly, it requires integrity to this purpose. When you control your life-brand with integrity and intention, while not eliminating them, you are giving the haters, dark forces and trolls a thick mental barrier to get to you. This deep confidence can be reached when life-brand is truly understood, embraced, controlled and shaped through the course of your life. They key is to possess life-brand awareness as early as the time we start creating our first social media account, maybe even sooner. The earlier in life we control our life-brand, the stronger our self-belief and confidence will grow.

Another confidence driver is to follow other life-brand owners that act and speak with the intention to uplift one another and spread positivity, rather than social media influencers that might not make us feel good, appreciated, or valued. I am speaking out of experience because I receive a lot of love, encouragement, and support from people in my social communities, so I choose with intention who to follow.

This brings me to another matter that requires your courage and confidence: how you may deal with any of your past public unintentional behaviors or language once it is analyzed and called-out for not being in alignment with your purpose. Addressing misaligned behavior and language asks for courage. Owning past mistakes publicly will increase life-brand awareness so others can refrain from making the same missteps. We are all human; we all make mistakes, but we have the opportunity to let others learn from it. This is what life-brand is all about.

Self-Awareness and Confidence

Controlling your life-brand can have a significant positive impact on your character development, especially when controlled early in life. The knowledge and awareness of the concept of life-brand enables you to develop strong self-awareness through the understanding of the impact your words and behavior can have on others.

Expressing your identity in alignment with your purpose will guide you toward sensitivity for your chosen behavior and language in public settings, as well as social media. It allows you to consciously choose how to express yourself to portray your true identity and authenticity. Most importantly, it enables you to understand what impact a word or gesture can have on relationships with others in the real and virtual world.

With self-awareness through controlling your life-brand comes self-confidence. A strong belief in your purpose gives you deep self-belief and confidence that positions you to go through life knowing your impact and life-brand voice drive positive change. Imagine having to deal with criticism from "haters" when you know at the same time how many people you are positively impacting in your life—it will seem so much less significant to receive criticism from people that disagree with you or try to bully you online.

As mentioned earlier, life-brand is also about giving back to your social media community. That could be a simple word of encouragement, sharing a post, or leaving a like. Life-brand is about bringing positivity into your own life and into other people's lives. Returning to girls and young women having the biggest challenges maneuvering the social media world these days, the key is to uplift other females around us, so they can follow our life-brand footsteps, feel good about themselves, and boost their confidence and self-belief. If we are living in integrity with our purpose and intentionally choosing our actions and words to drive positive change, so that other females can be inspired by us, the social media landscape will slowly start to shift. We will see a paradigm shift that is required to support girls and young women of Generation Brand to build early confidence and self-belief in their abilities before entering the workforce.

Leadership Skills

Besides allowing us to develop self-awareness and self-confidence, which are both crucial traits for a leader, life-brand also allows us to develop another set of unique skills that sets us apart from others who have not taken control of their life-brands.

When life-brand is not controlled, leadership skills are usually acquired in the workplace over the course of one's career. McKinsey and Lean In defined the key challenge to closing the gender gap in the workplace as the "broken rung", a bottleneck in the female talent pipeline right at the first time step up to manager. Significantly more men get put into these positions in the first place, which keeps slimming the female population in the workforce as they move towards senior leadership and eventually C-level positions. This situation diminishes women's ability to develop critical managerial and leadership skills early in their career, which can significantly slow down their professional development and therefore chances to advance in the workplace and climb the corporate ladder. Life-brand gives young women the opportunity to build leadership skills early on and allows them to demonstrate them in the workplace even prior to being in managerial positions.

Controlling life-brand teaches us the following crucial leadership skills:

- Integrity and Commitment
- Relationship Building
- Influencing Skills
- Communication Skills

Integrity and Commitment

The concept of life-brand is closely connected to the concept of integrity. We will be looking at life-brand integrity from two different angles based upon the following definitions:

"The quality or state of being complete or undivided."
—Merriam Webster Dictionary

"Always behaving according to the moral principles that you believe in, so that people respect and trust you."
—Macmillan Dictionary

Integrity being defined as a "state of being complete or undivided" correlates with the alignment of purpose and identity shaping a strong and controlled life-brand. You can only have a controlled life-brand if your purpose and the identity become one, act in sync, reflect each other, and become whole, in the sense that public language and behavior are fully intentional and reflect your identity in life.

Integrity also refers to "the quality of always behaving according to the moral principles that you believe in". Moral principles and life-brand purpose are closely connected. Acting and speaking in full alignment to your purpose allows you to shape a positive public perception based on "respect and trust" your audience has in you.

Choosing to live in integrity with your life-brand is a life-long commitment. The more public your life-brand becomes, the more followers you will attract. This ultimately leads to your life-brand voice reaching more and more people. Influencing many people through your life-brand voice comes with great respon-sibility to be fully aligned to your purpose and to act and speak reflecting your true identity. It's about being intentional and un-derstanding how many people your life-brand touches. Living and breathing full life-brand integrity gives you true self-belief, confidence, self-awareness, and courage to fully stand behind the positive impact you are having.

Practicing integrity and commitment with every public in-teraction, be it through language or behavior, on social media or in real life, enables you to transfer these characteristics onto oth-er areas in your life such as work, friends, or your family. Living a life driven by integrity and commitment allows you to achieve your goals faster, because you will stick to what you committed to in the first place (be it losing those 5 lbs., to start that blog you always spoke about, or to go back to school in your 40s). It helps you to honor your word and the promises you make to yourself and others. Simply put, it helps you to "walk the walk".

Also, acting and speaking with integrity to your purpose and identity will help you handle social media criticism you might receive. Rather than having a quick and unintentional reaction that does not reflect your identity, you will be able to step back, think, and then decide what the right course of action is. In most cases, it'll probably be ignorance, unless you receive feedback or criticism from someone who delivers it with intention and care (that would encourage a thoughtful response). Our reactions to criticism are as much part of our life-brand as content we share and will be captured in the cloud forever.

Relationship Building

Building and controlling your life-brand will expose you to other individuals in the real and virtual world. Using social media channels will allow you to reach many people that will be impacted by your life-brand voice, it will permit you to build relationships with people you might have never met otherwise (and a virtual relationship counts…we all learned that in 2020). Also, in order to strengthen your life-brand voice, to drive change and to reach a larger audience, you need to establish a network of people or have a community of followers. Over time, this tribe, community or network will allow you to give back, to help and support others, and to grow closer with some of the people in your virtual social circle. Virtual relationship building should not replace socializing in the real world; it should be seen as an addition to developing this crucial skill.

Influencing Skills

In order to drive change through your life-brand, you will have to inspire others to come on board with your purpose through your life-brand voice. You will influence them to follow you and your life-brand. Possessing strong influencing skills will allow you to equally excite others about your purpose and support you and your mission. Being a strong influencer is a critical leadership skill. If I look at my own career path and specifically the field I work in, I must influence others all the time. That could be executives or leadership peers in my organization or someone that comes to me and seeks advice on how to handle a particular challenge. I am not *telling* them what to do, I am positively influencing the decision-making process or someone's mindset. Influencing others is also linked to having the empathy to understand what encourages them, so you can help them rise and develop their true potential.

Being a life-brand "influencer" means to have the ability to positively impact other's behaviors, their decision-making process, mindset, and opinion through your social media life-brand voice. It does not mean that you are pushing people in a certain direction or that you control or manipulate the people in your social community. Life-brand influencers have a sense for what others care about and what their purpose is; they are able to influence others to start taking control of their life-brand, or at least be aware of it.

Influencing your social media community also means to be passionate and enthusiastic about your purpose. Influence can only happen when others feel your excitement and that you truly care about your purpose. It will attract followers that you want to attract.

Communication Skills

Communication skills can mean a lot of different things. In the context of life-brand, you will be able to develop the following:

- Understanding of the impact of your word/behavior

- Public speaking skills

- Written communication

Understanding the impact of unintentional language and the

impact of a misaligned identity and purpose will enable you to cultivate strong communication skills understanding how words are perceived by others, how they can be interpreted, and how much power they can wield if not used intentionally. When controlling your life-brand and being on the path of fully committing to align purpose and identity, you will be able to learn how words are landing with your audience, especially when using social media channels. Having an open mind, listening to (but not taking to heart) feedback and also public criticism can be instrumental to understanding how your words can be received in public settings, so you slowly learn how to adjust your choice of words to align closer to your identity. Building strong communication skills and learning how to properly express your identity through action and language is a journey life-brand will allow you to take.

Life-brand will also teach you public speaking skills. Especially if you love to make video contributions to your life-brand, you will develop early skills on how to address your audience, so they won't just hear you, but see you and enrich their experience by watching your enthusiasm and excitement you have about your purpose. Being able to record yourself and listening back to your words before sharing a video online will also make you more self-aware of every word you speak, which is a crucial skill to have for strong public speaking.

Writing posts, comments, articles, blog posts etc. with intention, will also sharpen your written communication skills. It will allow you to bring things to the point quickly, to be intentional about what you write, and how it could land with your audience. Cultivating solid written communication skills early in life will be extremely helpful as you advance your career.

Confidence Hacks

Make time for yourself. Bake it into your routine. Meditate or start the day with a yoga workout. If you cannot fit it into your workday alone, get other people involved! (I started a relaxation club at my last company where we meditated together three times per week for twenty minutes in the afternoon.)

8

Generation Brand

"I grew up in a physical world, and I speak English. The next generation is growing up in a digital world, and they speak social."

—Angela Ahrendts, former VP, Apple

As part of the research for this book, I was looking into the process of how generations were named and how generational cohorts were defined. I was surprised to learn that according to Pew Research's *Trend Magazine,* "no official commission or group decides what each generation is called and when it starts and ends. Instead, different names and birth year cutoffs are proposed, and through a somewhat haphazard process a consensus slowly develops in the media and popular parlance."

The following generational cohort names have been officially adopted by the public and are widely accepted by analysts and research centers:

Baby Boomers: born between 1946 to 1964

The Baby Boomers are considered to be the most well-defined of all the generations in the 20th century, they were named after the post-World War II spike in the birthrate that began in the mid-1940s. Baby Boomers are preceding Gen X and are often parents to kids of that cohort. They account for about 72 million people.

Gen X: born between 1965 and 1980

The term "Generation X" started to be adopted only in the early 1990s after author Douglas Coupland published his novel, *Generation X: Tales for an Accelerated Culture,* in 1991. Adults of Gen X are approaching the middle of their working careers and potential peak-earning years now and account for about 65 million people.

Millennials: born between 1981–1996

The 72 million people born following Gen X were tried to be named Gen Y on multiple occasions, but the name did not stick with the public. It took until 2000, when the authors Neil Howe and William Strauss published *Millennials Rising*, that the name was eventually widely accepted.

Gen Z: born after 1996

It is not entirely clear who to credit this name to, the term "Generation Z" appeared in several books over the years. In 2019, PEW Research Center surveyed several names for this generation to identify which name was widely accepted in the US and deemed Gen Z to be the most popular, so both *Merriam-Webster* and *Oxford* have adopted the name in their dictionaries. Most members of Gen Z are the children of Gen X and sometimes Millennials. No chronological endpoint has been set by researchers for this generational cohort as of yet, although 2012 started to surface as a suggested cut of year.

While there are suggested generation cohort names following Gen Z, researchers and analysts have not officially adopted any date range or cohort name as of yet for the generation born after 2012. The Center for Generational Kinetics defined a generation as "...a group of people born around the same time and raised around the same place. People in this birth cohort exhibit similar characteristics, preferences, and values over their lifetimes." Looking at recent generations, the Millennials started to experience the slow rise of digital with the internet being made available to the public in 1991, but only making it to most households years later. Kids and young adults of Gen Z on the other hand were raised in the age of digitalization with YouTube being launched in 2005, closely followed by Facebook opening its digital doors a year later, the first iPhone being released in 2007, and Instagram entering the stage in 2010, followed by other social media platforms and channels soon after.

Comparing Millennial with Gen Z daily social media usage, both generations show similar behavior. In the US, we are seeing up to 3 hours spent every day on social channels. In the Middle East and Africa, as well as Latin America, we even see up to 4 hours of daily social media usage these days. Especially Instagram usage for both generations is up by 17% from 2016 to 2019, stated a data roundup by Statista on December 7, 2019.

While we cannot predict social media usage trends for the children of Generation Brand as of yet, we know they are the first generation to be surrounded by social media since day one of their life because their parents spend significant hours of each day on these platforms.

I consider social media not just to be the main driver behind shaping the values and preferences of Generation Brand. I particularly consider social media to be a common nominator for generations to come growing up in the age of digital possibly overpowering any other generational characteristics of the future. Social media will determine this generation's life-brands, now even earlier than ever due to them being exposed to social media by their parents since infancy.

Generation Brand
[/jen-uhr-rAY-shuhn/ /brAnd/]

noun

> the generational cohort of individuals born between 2012 and 2030; the first-ever generation entirely exposed to uncontrolled life-brand creation from birth.

At its core, the education on the concept of life-brand will ultimately serve as education about safe social media usage for Millennials, Gen Z, and Generation Brand. There are many predictions on what the future of social media might look like in the year 2030. PEW Research has published a full range of expert opinions ranging from the rise of new social platforms possibly focusing on higher privacy standards, new legislation and regulation to ensure security, and even stronger polarization of social media over other media. Besides all of these predictions, one thing is clear. Social media is not going away. In order to facilitate a social media landscape shift, users *themselves* will have to be in the driver's seat of this significant change and controlling our life-brand will put us right in that position!

Besides a guide to safe social media usage, life-brand also serves as a vehicle for girls of Generation Brand, as well as established Millennial and Gen Z professional females, to build strong confidence and self-belief. Millennial and Gen Z professional women hold the power to encourage and inspire one another to control their life-brands, so their positive influence reaches the girls and soon-to-be young women of Generation Brand.

Figure 4 demonstrates the positive impact a controlled life-brand can have on (young) women of the Millennial cohort, Gen Z, Generation Brand as well as the following generations. When life-brand is controlled, a purpose has been identified (i.e. a passion, an idea, an interest etc.) and there is awareness of how women want to be perceived by the public.

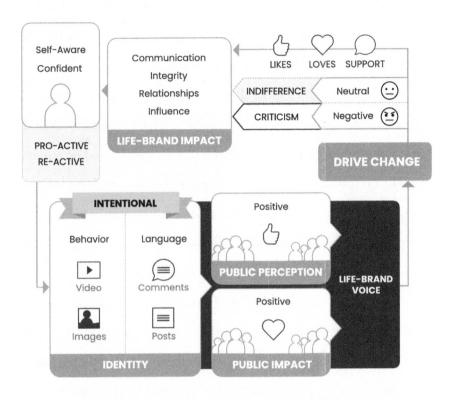

Figure 4. Women with a Controlled Life-Brand

They are active on social media platforms and understand how to display pro- and re-active language and behavior through comments, posts, images and videos that are in alignment with their purpose and truly reflect their identity. Their social media activity creates a positive impact on others and triggers a positive perception of their identity amongst their social media community and possibly beyond. Through these efforts they start to slowly build a life-brand voice that gets stronger and stronger over the course of their lifetime as they progress their education and career, turning women into life-brand role models for female peers and the following generations.

The public could have three types of reactions to women's social media presence. They will likely receive likes and loves and possibly support for their chosen purpose, there could be a neutral or no reaction to their social media presence, and they might also receive criticism from followers (possibly even backlash, cyberbullying or insults). Controlling a strong life-brand will not take the possibility away for them to encounter controversy. That being said, the education of life-brand, the confidence standing behind their purpose, and becoming part of a community of other life-brand owners will equip women to take cyber backlash less personal. As mentioned earlier, controlling their life-brands also allows women to develop or enhance leadership skills that will ultimately leave them more self-aware and confident obtaining an education, starting their journey in the workplace, or advancing their careers.

For this scenario to become a reality, women of the Millennial and Gen Z cohorts will have to lead the charge controlling their own life-brands, so girls and young women of Generation Brand are able to enter a social media environment that celebrates strong established female life-brands that serve as inspiration for the next generation.

Generation Brand: The Cultural Paradigm Shift

While the expression "paradigm shift" is scientific in nature, it has been adopted to describe "an important change that happens when the usual way of thinking about or doing something is replaced by a new and different way" (*Marriam-Webster*). In that sense, we refer to it as a *cultural paradigm shift*. Cultural paradigm shifts can have different origins. In the case of Generation Brand, we are looking at a change of belief in gender equality initiated through the power and reach of life-brand driven by women of the Millennial and Gen Z cohort. This shift is not a serendipitous occurrence, it is a controlled and conscious effort to impact Generation Brand's belief system and characteristics from an early age to shape a generation of confident and empowered females that feel equal to their male counterparts. Generation Brand's cultural paradigm shift starts with small changes rather than big leaps. Millennial and Gen Z women in the workforce building strong life-brand voices will lead a cultural revolution towards gender equality and a fundamental transformation in how men and women perceive themselves and their abilities.

For this generational paradigm shift to occur, the following prerequisite is necessary:

1. Consistent education of men and women, as well as boys and girls, of the Millennial, Gen Z, and Generation Brand cohorts on the concept of life-brand.

2. Professional women of the Millennial and Gen Z cohorts are collectively controlling their life-brands transforming the social media landscape and ultimately the perception of females' abilities and potential with a chosen purpose inspiring Generation Brand to follow their lead.

3. Life-brand to become the vehicle for females of Generation Brand to build strong confidence and self-belief as well as early leadership skills positioning them powerfully for their educational and career path to create equal opportunities for themselves compared to their male peers.

With Millennial and Gen Z women taking the lead, future professional women of Generation Brand will be uniquely positioned to create equal career opportunities for themselves (Figure 5).

A young woman of Generation Brand entering the workforce and going through the first few years of her career has developed a controlled life-brand with aligned purpose and identity

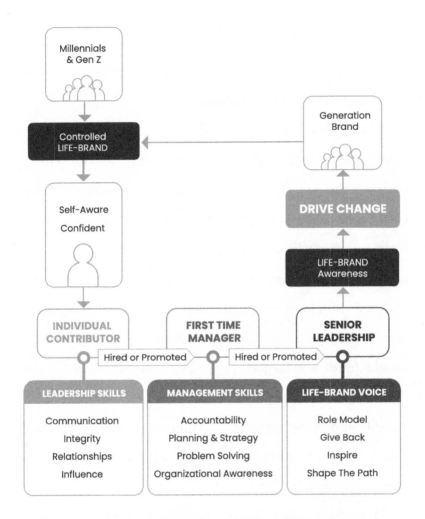

Figure 5. Generation Brand: Cultural Paradigm Shift

through her social media channels for years. Furthermore, she started to establish a life-brand voice that drives positive impact and change in her community. Thanks to these efforts, she has established strong communication skills, integrity, relationship building abilities, and influencing skills she would not have been able to present at this stage in her career as an individual contributor due to the lack of leadership and managerial opportunities to develop them in the workplace.

These skills have left her self-aware and confident in her abilities, not shying away from self-promotion thanks to the experience she gained through promoting her purpose through social media. She is now able to position herself equal to her male counterparts, displaying the same confidence, self-belief and comfort to self-promote as she reaches the "broken rung", as McKinsey and Lean In coined it, at the step up to first-time manager. Besides portraying the right skills to be considered a great candidate for a management position, she now also can show evidence of her leadership skills through the experience she has gained promoting her purpose publicly through social media (think about how confident she will walk into the interview for that manager job!).

Once the broken rung is successfully overcome, she now has the ability to continue to build her leadership skills through her life-brand, but also add valuable management skills such as being able to hold others accountable, planning and strategizing, solving problems, as well as having organizational awareness (these will vary and extend depending on her profession). As she progresses her way to senior leadership, her life-brand voice will gain more and more power and she will be able to reach other females that were in her shoes.

When Problems Solve Problems

As part of this book, we have discussed two problems: social media's negative impact on the current and following generations

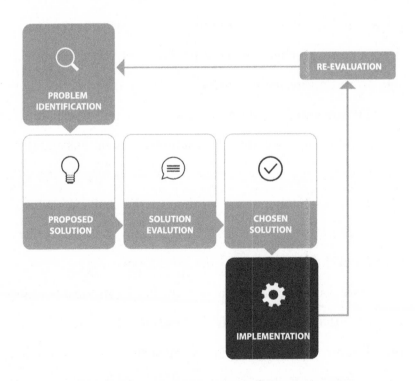

Figure 6. Classic Problem-Solving Approach

(especially females) and the gender gap in the workplace. Both problems are known for some time and have been partly addressed with proposed solutions. Yet none of these have actually been shown to solve these challenges for good due to the sheer global impact of these problems; they both seem overwhelming!

Classic problem-solving approaches can come in many shapes and forms, but broadly speaking, cover the following steps shown in Figure 6.

There have been many proposed solutions that address narrowing and eventually closing the gender gap with companies driving a stronger female talent pipeline, yet we have not seen significant improvement to achieve the goal to this point. There are also suggested solutions to address current social media trends and its negative impact on younger generations and their mental well-being such as stricter regulations to protect users. Those will absolutely positively influence the challenge at hand, yet we are not able to predict if these solutions actually drive a behavioral change in social media users themselves.

Figure 7 outlines a new approach that I call "The Solution Lifecycle" that simultaneously tackles both problems. This approach shows how one problem can most effectively be solved by connecting it to another, so the problems and the solution start to create a life cycle on their own that continuously feeds itself without needing constant reactivation. It counters quick peeks of enthusiasm, excitement, and a rapid short-lived push for change, and instead lets the process of the Solution Lifecycle emerge, grow, and gain strength over time.

The two challenges at hand are social media impact on young females, their mental state, confidence and self-belief, as well as the current lack of gender parity in the workplace. Millennial and Gen Z professional females controlling their life-brands on

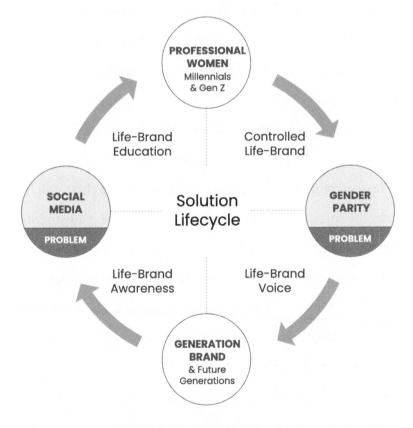

Figure 7. The Solution Lifecycle

a larger scale, will significantly increase confidence, empower-ment, and courage to reach for career opportunities with self-be-lief feeling equal to male counterparts. It will enable these profes-sional women to reach leadership and executive levels, positively impacting gender parity in business.

Actively controlled life-brands will allow professional wom-en to build their life-brand voice through various social media channels, reaching girls and soon-to-be young female adults of Generation Brand. Females of Generation Brand, in turn, are de-veloping life-brand awareness from an early age as they join the social media community thanks to the numerous role models they have access to.

What follows is a thorough social media and life-brand edu-cation possibly as part of Generation Brand's school curriculum to further reinforce this concept and to prepare them safely to enter the social media community when they are ready to inten-tionally maneuver it. Early life-brand awareness and education of Generation Brand (and beyond) will lay the foundation for a wave of confident female professionals that are entering the workforce with belief in their abilities and leadership potential.

This first wave of Millennial and Gen Z professional women with strong controlled life-brands will, over time, advance to se-nior leadership and executive positions equal to their male peers.

This development will strengthen their life-brand voices reaching more and more girls and young females with their chosen purpose, encouraging them to follow their lead. We discussed mentorship and sponsorship earlier in this book. Sponsorship cannot happen from afar; it requires close career involvement and vested support from the actual sponsor. Mentorship, on the other hand, in the form of encouragement, inspiration, and career advice can now happen through female professionals' life-brand voices thanks to the Solution Lifecycle. It will close the interim gap of female mentors in the workplace and make strong female life-brand role models accessible to all females that established a social media presence.

Both problems will start to solve each other through the power of one ongoing, never-ending solution. The true solution to both problems lies in using one problem to fix the other to drive an irreversible cultural paradigm shift towards gender equality for the generations to come.

Closing Thoughts

I always made an effort to support other women in my life, be it at work or in my community. I have also hired and promoted many women (and men!) throughout my (still early) professional journey; mentored and developed them to my best ability. I have always believed in social, economic, and political equality of the sexes and thought what I did in my day-to-day life was enough to make a contribution to this challenge. Building my own life-brand around the purpose of gender equality helped me to reach and impact even more women looking for inspiration, a little nudge to step out of their comfort zone and evolve, or simply provide guidance on how to accelerate their careers.

I have to state that while I know cultural patriarchy is something many women face in the workplace these days, that gender biases still significantly impact women's careers, and that women mentors and sponsors are rare (I only had male sponsors myself), I do not feel that my gender was ever in the way to advance my own career, putting me at a disadvantage. Quite the opposite. Of course, I am speaking about my personal situation and I am sure yours might look different, but it is still worth mentioning because I have worked across three continents, for several companies/brands, large and small. What I do relate to my gender "disadvantage" though is a confidence dip when it comes to asking for what I deserved earlier in my career, an anxiety to ask for a salary increase I knew was justified, and a feeling of male peers being more qualified than me although I knew I would do a way better job than some of them. Yet, I was not capable of portraying that.

As confident as I consider myself to be, I recall a conversation I had with my husband a few years back that really brought the problem home for me. I was preparing for an upcoming annual review and was writing down my accomplishments and areas to develop. As always, I would put some thought into it, so I could be prepared for the conversation with my boss. While I was taking notes, my husband sat down at the table and said: "You are asking for a promotion, right?" All he got was a blank stare. "What?" I replied. "You are asking for a promotion? How could you not after the year you just had?" That was the exact moment where it hit me. Big time. He was totally right. I had worked extremely hard, had a whole range of accomplishments to present, yet wasn't even *thinking* about asking for what was the obvious. I needed a moment to realize what was happening. He kept asking "Why are you not asking for a promotion?" I had no answer. I really did not know at the time. The only thing I knew was that he would have asked for one, so why didn't I? Why is he so much more confident in his abilities than I am?

I have been brought up by parents that have instilled confidence, self-belief, and trust in me since a very early age. I have been extremely lucky to grow up in a family like that and yet, it wasn't enough. It has been mainly the male influences throughout my life and career that have built and manifested my own confidence in my skills, capabilities and potential over the course of my career. Those men also sponsored me, and gave me opportunities based on my potential, even though I probably wasn't ready yet. There is a reason why I am saying this. I truly believe that *most* of us women (I am referring to Millennial and Gen Z female professionals) will encounter the occasional jerk—yes, so did I—the one man who will think you can't do the job that he does because you are a woman. Generally speaking, we encounter professional men that do not care if they hire a man or a woman; they just want to hire who is best for the job.

I think it's fair to say that companies are supportive of women making it to senior leadership and beyond. But driving full gender parity at all levels across organizations comes down to *us*…and I am directly speaking to the women who have picked up this book: own your career, own the opportunities that come your way, be courageous, and inspire other women around you.

The paradigm shift of Generation Brand needs us to actively own our life-brands so we can change the current social media landscape. With that being said, males are as much part of closing the gender gap as women are. Closing the gender gap means gender parity, equality. It cannot just happen with female input—it requires both genders to be on the same page.

You might put this book down and think, *that's a little much,*

I don't need to control my life-brand, I have done pretty well so far without doing so. Trust me, I get it. I wasn't even aware of this concept until a few years back. I gave zero intention to what I posted on social media and especially not what videos or photos were taken when we were out and about having fun with friends and just being teenagers, students and young adults. It didn't even cross my mind until I heard more and more about young adults being cancelled over severe social media missteps. That was the time when I actively started to control my life-brand and chose my purpose to be my profession (my passion has since then also become part of my life-brand).

My intention is not to turn every reader into a committed life-brand owner, although my hope is some readers will become just that. That being said, with the ease and access to post on various social channels so abundant, the chances of making a mistake are very real. Having life-brand awareness is your only protection. My hope is, at a minimum, that is what stuck with you. I cannot stress the importance enough for you to think back to the broken plate analogy I talked about earlier. You will be able to put your life-brand back together just like my mum did with that plate I broke, but only if you fully own up to whatever you did or said that broke it in the first place. But the life-brand cracks will remain. Forever.

While this sounds obvious, I would like to you to take away the following: *You only have **ONE** life-brand.* Yes, one. If you screw this one up, there won't be another.

Life-Brand

Launch Kit

This *Life-Brand Launch Kit* is the work section of this book that you can start completing once the motivation kicks in to fully control your life-brand. It will allow you to be self-analytical, to understand your current social media behavior, and it will enable you to define what your identity and life-brand purpose look like. The launch kit will include thought-provoking questions, to-do's and suggestions. I recommend working on these sections *in order* to truly kick off your life-brand journey from awareness to execution.

SECTION I

Understand Your Current Life-Brand

IRINA SORIANO

Objective

To start your intentional life-brand efforts, you need to gain awareness of what your current life-brand looks like. This part of the launch kit will require some self-analysis and behavior tracking so you can gain a great understanding where you are in your life-brand journey. We will use average estimates to understand your life-brand, which will help you to gain a rough picture.

1. Social Media Activities

List all your life-time social media activities (Twitter, Facebook, Instagram, TikTok, LinkedIn, Pinterest etc.). Please note, you should only write down the accounts that are or were active, meaning that you use or have used to engage in the social community.

SOCIAL MEDIA ACCOUNT	JOINED SINCE	PUBLIC
		YES ○ NO ○
		YES ○ NO ○
		YES ○ NO ○
		YES ○ NO ○
		YES ○ NO ○
		YES ○ NO ○
		YES ○ NO ○
		YES ○ NO ○
		YES ○ NO ○
		YES ○ NO ○

TOTAL NUMBER OF ACCOUNTS*

NUMBER OF YEARS SINCE FIRST ACTIVE SOCIAL MEDIA ACCOUNT WAS CREATED*

We will use this data in section I part 3

2. Social Media Diary

Over the next 7 days, complete the social media usage diary. I recommend picking a week where you can be very conscious of your behavior and have time to make some quick notes as you go through your day.

- **Column 1:** Write down the number of different social media platforms you visited that day.

- **Column 2:** Be as specific as possible on how much time you spent in total on all social media platforms that day.

- **Column 3:** Note how many likes and loves you have left on posts that day.

- **Column 4:** Note how many comments you have left on other people's posts.

- **Column 5:** Note how many individual posts you have (re) shared today across all platforms (that could just be text based, a picture, a video, a reel etc.).

Calculate the total for each column at the bottom for your personal awareness. Also calculate your total number of weekly comments and posts, we will use this number later.

	1 PLATFORMS VISITED	2 HOURS/ MINUTES	3 LIKES & LOVES	4 COMMENTS	5 POSTS
DAY 1					
DAY 2					
DAY 3					
DAY 4					
DAY 5					
DAY 6					
DAY 7					
TOTAL:					
TOTAL COMMENTS & POSTS:*					

We will use this data in section I part 3

3. Life-Brand Content

Next, you will estimate how much content you have publicly contributed to your life-brand. Use some of the previous data you collected about your social media usage to complete the following boxes below. Multiply all of the numbers you collected and calculate the estimated total amount of social media content you have produced during your lifetime. This number is a rough estimate but gives you a decent idea of where you stand. There is no "good" or "bad" outcome, the goal is to create awareness of how much content you have publicly shared with the world (possibly without intention).

Total number of weekly comments and posts combined (total column 4 and 5 from your diary)

◯

X

52 WEEKS

X

Total number of past and active social media accounts

◯

X

Number of years since you created your first active social media account

◯

=

Total public life-brand contributions

◯

4. Understand your life-brand content

Now you know roughly **how much** content you have shared with the world over the course of your social media life, we will look into **what** type of content you shared (as far as you can track it). You will probably not be able to review all your past comments ever made, but you should have access to all social media posts you shared with the world (unless deleted). Set some time aside and skim through all your active social media accounts and review every single post you shared all the way back to post number one. Answer the following awareness questions.

Did you ever share any content that the public might have perceived as controversial, daring, or inappropriate for you or your age?

(If unsure, you will likely be able to tell by your community's reaction.)

YES ☐   **NO** ☐

If yes, how often?

☐ ONCE OR TWICE

☐ UP TO 10 TIMES

☐ UP TO 50 TIMES

☐ ON A REGULAR BASIS

Did you ever receive criticism, backlash, or cyber-bullying online after posting?

YES ☐   **NO** ☐

If yes, how did this make you feel?

_____

_____

_____

_____

Do you feel all your posts reflect you and your true identity, the real you?

YES   **NO**

Why?

_____

_____

_____

_____

_____

_____

When reviewing posts, did you see a trend of what you post about? Look for a possible "purpose" or a topic that keeps resurfacing.

(We will be able to use this later on.)

_____

_____

_____

_____

_____

_____

_____

Notes

IRINA SORIANO

SECTION II

Define Your Life-Brand Purpose and Identity

IRINA SORIANO

Objective

Now you have a better understanding what your current life-brand looks like, we will start to define your identity and discover your life-brand purpose. Your purpose will likely evolve and change over time.

1. Define Your Identity

We will now define your identity, what you stand for, and what you would describe as your authentic self. This part of your life-brand starter kit requires a little more time, do not rush through these sections and allow time to think and reflect.

In three short statements, describe the "real you".
(Hint: you can also ask friends and family what they think.)

Example: I am compassionate and truly care for other people's well-being.

1. _____

_____

_____

_____

_____

2. _____

_____

_____

_____

_____

3. _____

_____

_____

_____

_____

_____

Looking at past social media posts you made, how many speak against or do not support this defined identity?

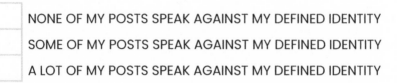

NONE OF MY POSTS SPEAK AGAINST MY DEFINED IDENTITY

SOME OF MY POSTS SPEAK AGAINST MY DEFINED IDENTITY

A LOT OF MY POSTS SPEAK AGAINST MY DEFINED IDENTITY

Note

We discussed that social media posts and comments can be deleted but remain in the cloud forever. After understanding how much your social media behavior reflects or does not reflect your identity, you might still want to consider at least removing content from your accounts before moving on.

2. Discover Your Purpose

In this section we will try to find what possible purpose you could build your life-brand on. This will be a little bit of a process, so don't feel discouraged if you cannot define your purpose yet. Go through each of the sections. If you answer YES, please continue answering the follow up questions (even if you score several yesses). If you answer NO, just move on to the next possible purpose. This is the time to be creative, consider what might seem silly, unheard of, or irrelevant. No limitations, please!

PASSION

Is there something in your life that you deeply care about? Think about a topic you might be speaking or reading a lot about.

YES ☐   **NO** ☐

If you answered yes: What is the topic? Try to keep it to a sentence.

_____

_____

_____

_____

_____

_____

How long have you been passionate about this topic?

_____

_____

_____

_____

_____

_____

What do you think your contribution to this topic could be?

_____

_____

_____

_____

_____

_____

_____

_____

_____

_____

Why do you feel so passionate about it?

_____

_____

_____

_____

_____

_____

_____

_____

IDEA

Did you ever have an idea that might tackle a challenge or problem? Did you ever invent anything? Also consider ideas that might seem silly or crazy (those are the best ones!).

YES ☐   **NO** ☐

If you answered yes: What is the idea? Try to keep it to a sentence.

_____

_____

_____

_____

_____

_____

How does your idea address a challenge, a problem, an issue, or a need?

_____

_____

_____

_____

_____

_____

What audience could benefit from this idea?

_____

_____

_____

_____

_____

_____

_____

_____

_____

_____

Why is your idea something people should know about?

_____

_____

_____

_____

_____

_____

_____

_____

_____

_____

PROFESSION

Do you feel your profession motivates you to speak about it on a regular basis? If you had a career change, you could also consider a past profession or a potential future profession.

YES ☐   **NO** ☐

If you answered yes: What is the profession?

_____

_____

_____

_____

_____

_____

_____

How well are you recognized in your field of exper-tise by your professional community?

_____

_____

_____

_____

_____

What could other professionals learn from you?

_____

_____

_____

_____

_____

_____

_____

_____

_____

Why are you a great person to publicly speak about this profession?

_____

_____

_____

_____

_____

_____

_____

_____

_____

EXPERTISE

Are you an expert in a particular field? Think broad, this does not mean you are working in this field, you might have become an expert in your free time. Also, you might have a particular skill that sets you apart, something you know how to do really well.

YES ☐   **NO** ☐

If you answered yes: What is your expertise (or skill)? Try to keep it to a sentence.

_____

_____

_____

_____

_____

How have you become an expert and/or how have you developed this skill?

_____

_____

_____

_____

_____

What can people learn from you?

_____

_____

_____

_____

_____

_____

_____

_____

_____

_____

Why could others be interested in learning about your expertise?

_____

_____

_____

_____

_____

_____

_____

_____

_____

HOBBY

Do you have a hobby you spend your time with outside of school or work? This could be something you love doing and something you are excited about filling your time with.

YES ☐   **NO** ☐

If you answered yes: What is your hobby?

_____

_____

_____

_____

_____

_____

How have you gotten into your hobby?

_____

_____

_____

_____

_____

What does this hobby say about you and your identity?

_____
_____
_____
_____
_____
_____
_____
_____
_____
_____

Why do you love your hobby?

_____
_____
_____
_____
_____
_____
_____
_____
_____
_____

INTEREST

If you answered NO to all the previous yes/no questions, do not feel discouraged. You'll get there! Let's look at your possible interests. Please also complete this section, if you already had a few yesses, I want you to look at as many purpose options as possible. An interest can also mean that you have never pursued it before but wish to do so (your journey to learn something new can totally be a purpose).

Is there anything out there that you are interested in? Check with yourself:

- Is there something you like reading or hearing about (books, media, social...)?

- Is there something that occupies your mind on a regular basis?

- Is there a skill you wish you had? (Let's say you want to be able to bake, yet never baked a cookie in your life.)

YES   **NO**

If you answered yes: What is your interest?

_____

_____

_____

_____

_____

_____

_____

_____

How would it impact your life and the people in it if you were to pursue this interest?

_____

_____

_____

_____

_____

_____

_____

_____

_____

What do you need to do to pursue this interest: do you need resources, people that have to help you, is there a financial component etc.?

_____

_____

_____

_____

_____

_____

_____

_____

Why could you not pursue this interest?

_____

_____

_____

_____

_____

_____

_____

_____

BONUS: If you gave a reason to the previous question, brainstorm a solution (excuses and purpose
do not like each other very much).

3. Pick Your Purpose.

I am sure we got at least one YES to one of our purpose questions. If so, that is where you start. If you had several yesses, spend some time evaluating what purpose feels the "strongest".

Let's check your level of excitement about your purpose...

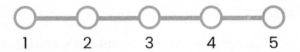

1   2   3   4   5

I am not
motivated at all
to post about my
purpose.

I cannot wait to
share my purpose
with my social media
community.

We need you to be at least at a 4 to get the ball rolling, otherwise I would encourage you to go back to the last section. Being excited, enthusiastic, and fired up about your purpose is required to bring other people on your life-brand journey with you and to inspire others around you to follow your lead owning their own life-brands. If you were able to pick your purpose, write it down.

My purpose is...

_____

_____

_____

_____

_____

_____

_____

_____

_____

_____

_____

4. Visualize Your Life-Brand

Complete the chart to visualize your life-brand. Snap a picture and have this visual with you at all times as a reminder before posting content on social media.

_____'s
Your name

Life-Brand

IDENTITY

My identity is defined as (3 words):

1. _____

2. _____

3. _____

PURPOSE

My Purpose is based on my

_____

My purpose is

_____

_____

_____

In the long-run, I wish for my life-brand voice to reach

_____

Specific audiences or communities

I want to impact change in/at

_____

Your workplace, school, community, city, state, country etc.

The change I wish to drive with my life-brand is

_____

_____

IRINA SORIANO

Notes

IRINA SORIANO

IRINA SORIANO

IRINA SORIANO

IRINA SORIANO

IRINA SORIANO

IRINA SORIANO

IRINA SORIANO

Endnotes

Introduction: Your Life-Brand

MacKay, Jory. "Screen time stats 2019: Here's how much you use your phone during the workday." RescueTime. March 21, 2019.

    https://blog.rescuetime.com/screen-time-stats-2018/#:~:text=When%20we%20looked%20at%20the,in%20excess%20 of%204.5%20hours

Fischer, Mark. "'I HATE GAY PEOPLE': Brewers pitcher Josh Hader's offensive tweets resurface during All-Star Game." New York Daily News. July 18, 2018.

    https://www.nydailynews.com/sports/baseball/ny-sports-josh-hader-racist-tweets-20180718-story.html

Ronson, Jon. "How One Stupid Tweet Blew Up Justine Sacco's Life." The New York Times Magazine. February 12, 2015.

    https://www.nytimes.com/2015/02/15/magazine/how-one-stupid-tweet-ruined-justine-saccos-life.html

Dimock, Michael. "Defining generations: Where Millennials end and Generation Z begins." Pew Research Center. January 17, 2019.

    https://www.pewresearch.org/fact-tank/2019/01/17/where-millennials-end-and-generation-z-begins/

Rideout, Vicky. "The Common Sense Census: Media Use by Teens and Tweens." Common Sense Media. 2015.

    https://www.commonsensemedia.org/sites/default/files/uploads/research/census_researchreport.pdf

Turner, Ash. "How Many People Have Smartphones Worldwide."

Bank My Cell. January 2021.

https://www.bankmycell.com/blog/how-many-phones-are-in-the-world

O'Dea, S. "Number of smartphone users worldwide from 2016 to 2021." Statista. December 10, 2020.

https://www.statista.com/statistics/330695/number-of-smartphone-users-worldwide/

Addiction Center. "Social Media Addiction."

https://www.addictioncenter.com/drugs/social-media-addiction/

Chapter 1: The Death of Privacy

Robb, Michael. "Tweens, Teens, and Phones: What Our 2019 Research Reveals." Common Sense Media. October 29, 2019.

https://www.commonsensemedia.org/blog/tweens-teens-and-phones-what-our-2019-research-reveals

Bologna, Caroline. "What's the Deal with Generation Alpha?" HuffPost. November 8, 2019.

https://www.huffpost.com/entry/generation-alpha-after-gen-z_l_5d420ef4e4b0aca341181574

Brennan, Jerry. "Future security career challenges in 2021 and beyond." Security. January 4, 2021.

https://www.securitymagazine.com/articles/94263-future-security-career-challenges-in-2021-and-beyond

Silver, Laura. "Smartphone Ownership Is Growing Rapidly Around the World, but Not Always Equally." Pew Research Center. February 5, 2019.

https://www.pewresearch.org/global/2019/02/05/smart-phone-ownership-is-growing-rapidly-around-the-world-but-not-always-equally/

Jacobo, Julia. "Teens spend more than 7 hours on screens for enter-tainment a day: Report." ABC News. October 29, 2019.

https://abcnews.go.com/US/teens-spend-hours-screens-en-tertainment-day-report/story?id=66607555

Kato, Brooke. "What is cancel culture? Everything to know about the toxic online trend." New York Post. July 10, 2020.

https://nypost.com/article/what-is-cancel-culture-breaking-down-the-toxic-online-trend/

Wilson, Mark. "People are failing hilariously at working from home." Fast Company. March 19, 2020.

https://www.fastcompany.com/90478967/farts-cats-naked-bodies-people-are-failing-hilariously-at-working-from-home

Robertson, Katie. "Jeffrey Toobin Is Fired by The New Yorker." The New York Times. November 11, 2020.

https://www.nytimes.com/2020/11/11/business/media/jef-frey-toobin-fired-new-yorker.html

Chapter 2: Chasing the Like

Perrin, Andrew, and Monica Anderson. "Share of U.S. adults using social media, including Facebook, is mostly unchanged since 2018." Pew Research Center. April 10, 2019.

https://www.pewresearch.org/fact-tank/2019/04/10/share-of-u-s-adults-using-social-media-including-facebook-is-most-ly-unchanged-since-2018/

Almendrala, Anna. "This Could Explain Why Teens Are So Obsessed with Social Media." HuffPost. June 3, 2016.

https://www.huffpost.com/entry/this-could-explain-why-teens-are-so-obsessed-with-social-media_n_574f7084e4b0ed593f134279

York University. "Study: Social media is affecting the way we view our bodies – and not in a good way." November 15, 2018.

https://news.yorku.ca/2018/11/15/study-social-media-is-affecting-the-way-we-view-our-bodies-and-not-in-a-good-way/

Anderson, Monica. "A Majority of Teens Have Experienced Some Form of Cyberbullying." Pew Research Center. September 27, 2018.

https://www.pewresearch.org/internet/2018/09/27/a-majority-of-teens-have-experienced-some-form-of-cyberbullying/

Cyberbullying.org.

https://cyberbullying.org

Gladden, Matthew, Alana M. Vivolo-Kantor, Merle E. Hamburger, Corey D. Lumpkin. "Bullying Surveillance Among Youths: Uniform Definitions for Public Health and Recommended Data Elements." Centers for Disease Control and United States Department of Education. 2014.

https://www.cdc.gov/violenceprevention/pdf/bullying-definitions-final-a.pdf

Chapter 3: All Shame, No Fame?

Nir, Sarah Maslin. "White Woman Is Fired After Calling Police on Black Man in Central Park." The New York Times. October 14, 2020.

https://www.nytimes.com/2020/05/26/nyregion/amy-coo-per-dog-central-park.html

Douthat, Ross. "10 Theses About Cancel Culture." The New York Times. July 14, 2020.
https://www.nytimes.com/2020/07/14/opinion/cancel-cul-ture-.html?searchResultPosition=3

Shead, Sam. "JK Rowling criticizes 'cancel culture' in open letter signed by 150 public figures." CNBC.com. July 8, 2020.
https://www.cnbc.com/2020/07/08/jk-rowling-cancel-cul-ture.html

Cole, Rachel. "Gilbert teen apologizes for racist TikTok that went viral." 12News.com. April 20, 2020.
https://www.12news.com/article/news/local/valley/gilbert-teen-apologizes-for-racist-tiktok-that-went-viral/75-ef-51c4bf-f33a-4ddf-ba88-ec73f8a19794

Levin, Dan. "A Racial Slur, a Viral Video, and a Reckoning." The New York Times. December 26, 2020.
https://www.nytimes.com/2020/12/26/us/mimi-groves-jim-my-galligan-racial-slurs.html

Stamm, Kathryn, and Luke Pichini. "Incoming Cornell Freshman Uses Racial Slur in Video, Loses Spot on Football Team." The Cornell Daily Sun. June 23, 2020.
https://cornellsun.com/2020/06/23/incoming-cornell-fresh-man-uses-racial-slur-in-video-loses-spot-on-football-team/

Marshall, Tara, Katharina Lefringhausen, Nelli Ferenszi. "The Big Five, self-esteem, and narcissism as predictors of the topics people write about in Facebook status updates." *ScienceDirect. Volume 85, October 2015, Pages 35-40.*

https://www.sciencedirect.com/science/article/pii/
S0191886915003025

Stein, Joel. "How Trolls Are Ruining the Internet." *Time. August 18, 2016.*

https://time.com/4457110/internet-trolls/

Kludt, Tom. "New York Times editor quits Twitter over anti-Semitic tweets." *CNNMoney.com. June 9, 2016.*

https://money.cnn.com/2016/06/08/media/new-york-times-
jon-weisman-twitter/

Morris, David. "Bestselling Feminist Author Jessica Valenti Quits Social Media After Rape and Death Threats Directed at Daughter." *Fortune. July 31, 2016.*

https://fortune.com/2016/07/31/bestselling-femi-
nist-author-jessica-valenti-quits-social-media-af-
ter-rape-and-death-threats-directed-at-daughter/

Rowlatt, Justin. "Climate change: Greta Thunberg calls out the 'haters'." *BBC.com. September 27, 2019.*

https://www.bbc.com/news/science-environment-49855980

Rosenberg, Eli. "A vegan YouTube star went to Bali. A video of her there brought her platform crashing down." *The Washington Post. March 22, 2019.*

https://www.washingtonpost.com/technology/2019/03/22/
vegan-youtube-star-rawvana-gets-caught-eating-meat-cam-
era/

Chapter 4: Digital Destiny of the Sexes

Huang, Jess, Alexis Krivkovich, Irina Starikova, Lareina Yee, and Delia Zanoschi. "Women in the Workplace." McKinsey & Company. October 2019.

https://www.mckinsey.com/~/media/McKinsey/Featured%20Insights/Gender%20Equality/Women%20in%20the%20Workplace%202019/Women-in-the-workplace-2019.pdf

Devillard, Sandrine, Alix de Zelicourt, Sandra Sancier-Sultan, and Cécile Kossoff. "Women Matter." McKinsey & Company. December 2016.

https://www.mckinsey.com/~/media/mckinsey/featured%20insights/women%20matter/reinventing%20the%20workplace%20for%20greater%20gender%20diversity/women-matter-2016-reinventing-the-workplace-to-unlock-the-potential-of-gender-diversity.ashx

Graf, Nikki, Anna Brown, and Eileen Patten. "The narrowing, but persistent, gender gap in pay." Pew Research Center. March 22, 2019.

https://www.pewresearch.org/fact-tank/2019/03/22/gender-pay-gap-facts/

Center on Education and the Workforce. "Women Can't Win." Georgetown University.

https://cew.georgetown.edu/cew-reports/genderwagegap/

Krivkovich, Alexis, Irina Stanikova, Kelsey Robinson, Rachel Valentino, Lareino Yee. "Women in the Workplace 2020." McKinsey & Company. September 30, 2020.

https://www.mckinsey.com/featured-insights/diversity-and-inclusion/women-in-the-workplace

Carbajal, Jose. "Patriarchal Culture's Influence on Women's Leadership Ascendancy." The Journal of Faith, Education and Community. 2018.

https://scholarworks.sfasu.edu/cgi/viewcontent.cgi?article=1011&context=jfec

Ibarra, Herminia. "A Lack of Sponsorship Is Keeping Women from Advancing into Leadership." Harvard Business Review. August 19, 2019.

https://hbr.org/2019/08/a-lack-of-sponsorship-is-keeping-women-from-advancing-into-leadership

Artz, Benjamin, Amanda Goodall and Andrew J. Oswald. "Research: Women Ask for Raises as Often as Men but Are Less Likely to Get Them." Harvard Business Review. June 25, 2018.

https://hbr.org/2018/06/research-women-ask-for-raises-as-often-as-men-but-are-less-likely-to-get-them

Harvard University. "Leaning Out: Teen Girls and Leadership Biases." July 2015.

https://mcc.gse.harvard.edu/reports/leaning-out

Lindeman, Meghan, Amanda Durik, and Maura Dooley. "Women and Self-Promotion: A Test of Three Theories." Sage. January 29, 2018.

https://journals.sagepub.com/doi/10.1177/0033294118755096

KPMG. "Women's Leadership Study." 2019.

https://assets.kpmg/content/dam/kpmg/ph/pdf/Thought-LeadershipPublications/KPMGWomensLeadershipStudy.pdf

Chapter 5: The Power of Life-Brand

Interview with Rushion McDonald. Zoom. November 13, 2020.

Chan, Wilfred. "Ariana Grande apologizes and explains doughnut licking." CNN. July 10, 2015.

> https://www.cnn.com/2015/07/09/entertainment/ariana-grande-donut-licking-america/index.html

Koblin, John. "After Racist Tweet, Roseanne Barr's Show Is Canceled by ABC." The New York Times. May 29, 2018.

> https://www.nytimes.com/2018/05/29/business/media/roseanne-barr-offensive-tweets.html

Wolfson, Sam. "Ambien maker responds to Roseanne Barr: 'Racism is not a known side effect'." The Guardian. May 30, 2018.

> https://www.theguardian.com/culture/2018/may/30/roseanne-ambien-racism-tweet-side-effect-response-sanofi

Alter, Charlotte, Suyin Haynes, and Justin Worland. "2019 Person of the Year: Greta Thunberg." Time. December 23, 2019.

> https://time.com/person-of-the-year-2019-greta-thunberg/

BBC. "'Shine theory': How women are plugging the gender gap." September 14, 2016.

> https://www.bbc.com/news/world-us-canada-37360233

Chapter 6: Life-Brand Awareness

CNN. "Tiger Woods' apology: Full transcript." February 19, 2010.

https://www.cnn.com/2010/US/02/19/tiger.woods.transcript/index.html

Rosen, Christopher. "Chris Rock Addresses Jimmy Fallon's Blackface Impression." *Vanity Fair. September 16, 2020.*

https://www.vanityfair.com/hollywood/2020/09/chris-rock-jimmy-fallon-blackface

Billings, Patrick. "Brisbane's alleged poo jogger resigns from corporate role." *The Courier Mail. June 7, 2018.*

https://www.couriermail.com.au/news/queensland/brisbanes-alleged-poo-jogger-resigns-from-corporate-role/news-story/54b10461c8d14018bdd7ffd05ab9e43d

BBC. "Jerry Falwell Jr to take leave of absence after racy photo." *August 7, 2020.*

https://www.bbc.com/news/world-us-canada-53703294

Chapter 7: Life-Brand Skills

Brown, Brené. "Dare to Lead Hub."

https://daretolead.brenebrown.com

Twenge, Jean. "How Are Generations Named?" *Trend Magazine. January 26, 2018.*

https://www.pewtrusts.org/en/trend/archive/winter-2018/how-are-generations-named

The Center for Generational Kinetics
https://genhq.com

J. Clement. "Instagram user share in the United States 2020, by age group." *Statista. December 7, 2020.*

https://www.statista.com/statistics/398166/us-instagram-user-age-distribution/

Vogels, Emily, Lee Rainie, and Janna Anderson. "The innovations these experts predict by 2030." Pew Research Center. June 30, 2020.

https://www.pewresearch.org/internet/2020/06/30/innovations-these-experts-predict-by-2030/

Merriam-Webster. "paradigm shift".

https://www.merriam-webster.com/dictionary/paradigm%20shift

IRINA SORIANO

About the Author

Irina Soriano is a German businesswoman currently working in the technology industry. She has lived and worked all over the world, from EMEA to Asia-Pacific and lastly, the US, which she now calls her home. Throughout her career, she has been extremely passionate about mentoring young women and men to maneuver their career paths, but she has especially invested time to encourage, inspire, and empower women to build the confidence to ask for what they desire and deserve. Irina has built a strong life-brand around her profession and decided that the year 2021 will be the opportunity to also establish her life-brand around what she cares most about—making a significant contribution to closing the gender gap in the workplace.

Irina lives in New York City with her husband, Chris. Generation Brand is her debut book.

Instagram: irina.soriano

Linkedin: irina-soriano

Facebook: irinasoriano.is